PRAISE FOR SCANNED

"Nick Corbishley exposes the intricate web spun by global predators using the principles of mass formation psychosis in order to drive an agenda of worldwide injection of biologically active substances. People entranced in fear and confusion feel their entire existence depends on periodic receipt of grossly unsafe and ineffective products—all to live the day-by-day existence they had grown to expect. Corbishley unwinds this madness into an understandable framework with chilling insights about the loss of medical freedom that is inextricably linked to loss of social and economic freedoms. This book is an emergency read."

— **Peter A. McCullough**, MD, MPH;
chief medical advisor, Truth for Health Foundation

"*Scanned* by Nick Corbishley is essential reading; this book explains in an incontrovertible way how 'vaccine passports' have already closed off basic human liberties in many parts of the formerly free world, and shines a light on the mounting layers of dystopia and control for which they form the foundation. No one should risk missing the information in this book."

— **Naomi Wolf**, *New York Times* best-selling author
of *The End of America* and *Outrages*

"'Show me your papers' is a phrase that should send chills down the spine of any thinking person. The idea that we would bar free citizens from access to public life because they have chosen to say, 'No, thank you' to a pharmaceutical intervention for religious, medical, or philosophical reasons is breathtakingly wrong. Nick Corbishley's outstanding new book, *Scanned*, explains why. Anyone who cares about public health and personal freedom needs this book."

— **Jennifer Margulis**, PhD, award-winning
science journalist and best-selling author

"The rollout of 'vaccine passports' and the broader pseudo-medical social-segregation system they are part of is among the most sinister and alarming threats we have faced in our lifetimes. Under the pretense of 'keeping us safe and healthy,' governments, supranational governing entities, and tech corporations have colluded to impose unprecedented restrictions and surveillance on people all around the world. *Scanned* unpacks the logical insanity of the official 'vaccine passport' narrative and describes how mass COVID hysteria has been instrumentalized to consolidate not only wealth and power, but biometric control over ordinary citizens."

—**C. J. Hopkins**, award-winning playwright,
novelist, and political satirist

SCANNED

Why Vaccine Passports and Digital IDs Will Mean the End of Privacy and Personal Freedom

Nick Corbishley

CHELSEA GREEN PUBLISHING
White River Junction, Vermont
London, UK

Project Manager: Patricia Stone
Developmental Editor: Brianne Goodspeed
Copy Editor: Nancy A. Crompton
Indexer: Nancy A. Crompton
Designer: Melissa Jacobson

Printed in the United States of America.
First printing February 2022.
10 9 8 7 6 5 4 3 2 1   22 23 24 25 26

ISBN 978-1-64502-162-9 (paperback) | ISBN 978-1-64502-163-6 (ebook)
| ISBN 978-1-64502-164-3 (audio book)

Library of Congress Cataloging-in-Publication Data is available upon request.

Chelsea Green Publishing
85 North Main Street, Suite 120
White River Junction, Vermont USA

Somerset House
London, UK

www.chelseagreen.com

CONTENTS

Introduction

By the time you open this book, there's a good chance you either already have some form of vaccine passport or are being strongly encouraged (to put it kindly) to get one. As of this writing, most countries in Europe, my continent of residence, have already implemented one, as have Australia, Canada, New Zealand, Japan, Uruguay, and Argentina.

Of course, the term "passport" is misleading. A passport is a document issued by a State that certifies the holder's citizenship and entitles them to travel under its protection to and from foreign countries. While it is true that immunity certificates for diseases such as smallpox and yellow fever have been around for over a century, they have always come in paper form whereas a vaccine passport is likely to come in the form of a digital document. Most important, vaccine passports have broader applications and darker implications than normal passports or immunity certificates. They can be required not only to establish identity or vaccine status at national borders but also to travel, access public buildings, qualify for basic services, and even to work within one's own country of residence.

To qualify for a vaccine passport in most jurisdictions, you need to be up to date on the COVID-19 vaccinations. In some places, such as the EU, a recent negative polymerase chain reaction (PCR) test may suffice. In the EU, unlike the United States and the United Kingdom, natural immunity is still considered a relevant scientific phenomenon, a fact that is partially reflected in the EU's vaccine passport legislation (or at least it was at the time of writing this). EU residents who have had an infection of COVID-19 can qualify for the passport, but for only a six-month period.

Unfortunately, even that didn't work out for me.

My wife and I came down with COVID-19 in late July 2021. We were both unvaccinated. Both of us, in our mid-forties, had reasonably mild symptoms—fever, fatigue, chills, cough, joint pains, lack of appetite, headaches—that lasted for about a week. Then we began a slow process of recovery. After around a month we were more or less back to normal. Both of us now have natural antibodies yet only one of us is eligible for the EU's vaccine passport—the so-called Green Pass.

Like thousands of other people in Spain, where I am a long-term resident, I was given the wrong test at the onset of symptoms. My wife, by contrast, took the correct one four days later, since she had tested negative the first time round. During Spain's big summer wave, many of the country's primary-care providers began using the much faster (and much cheaper) antigen tests to check patients for infection. The only problem is that to qualify for the EU's Green Pass on the grounds of natural infection, you need to have had a positive PCR test; the results of antigen tests like mine do not suffice.

That means that in the fall of 2021 there were thousands of people in Spain—myself included—who were in limbo. We have all had a COVID-19 infection, which means we should have some degree of immunity. And that means we should qualify for the EU's Green Pass, at least for a six-month window of time. But because Spain's health authorities used the wrong test in our cases, we don't. This includes people who spent weeks in a hospital fighting and recovering from the disease. According to the EU's official records none of us have had COVID-19. According to Spain's public health authorities, we have.

This is just one example of how arbitrary life can quickly become in the new reality that is fast taking shape around us. There are many more, as you will discover in this book. As governments exert ever greater power and authority over our lives, all it takes is a simple administrative mistake or algorithmic error or bias for everyday citizens to suddenly find themselves unable to travel, or even access public places and basic services in their hometowns. And as we've repeatedly seen since this pandemic began, governments and public authorities are prone to making mistakes quite often.

I am writing these words from my country-in-law, Mexico, on January 1, 2022. By the time this book is published, in mid-February, some of the details described herein will have undoubtedly changed.

In the COVID era the pace of change is so fast it is hard to keep up. In the space of six weeks a brand-new variant can emerge and get a foothold on more than one continent. Not only is the virus evolving and mutating all the time; so too is the response of governments, global institutions and corporations to it—faster than any individual can reasonably keep up with major decisions that impact their lives in many, and significant, ways.

These are just two of the numerous reasons why the rapid rollout of vaccine passports by governments around the world should give us serious pause, regardless of our vaccine status.

This Book Is for Everyone, Vaccinated or Not

Vaccinated or not, if you live in a city, country, or region that has rolled out a vaccine passport, or is in the process of doing so, this book is for you. It is a manifesto, not against the vaccines themselves, but against how they are being used to radically reorder society in ways that are of little benefit to anyone except the business, financial, and political elite. Whatever our beliefs about the vaccines themselves, we will all have to live with the consequences of the changes the passports and mandates will bring. Those consequences will include greater social division and polarization, loss of bodily autonomy, growing authoritarianism, further erosion of privacy, and the creation of a two-tiered society.

If you're fully vaccinated, it is arguably even more important that you read this book. You may assume you won't be affected by their roll out; after all, you've complied with all the public health requirements thus far. You have done what's been asked of you. But there's no guarantee that you'll meet additional requirements of the future. As anyone who has lived in an authoritarian state knows, rules and mandates have an annoying habit of multiplying.

For each and every one of us, the creation of a vaccine passport system will represent a before-and-after moment. A passport that isn't really a passport, for a vaccine that isn't really a vaccine, threatens to alter, irrevocably, the relationship between the government and the governed; between those who hold power and those over whom it is exercised. As the (pro-vaccine) award-winning journalist Glenn Greenwald points out, it risks converting "what have always been basic rights—to enter public places, fly, attend public gatherings—into state-granted privileges one earns through compliance with demands of political officials that one inject substances into one's own body."[1]

Regardless of how you feel about the vaccine itself, we should all oppose the current direction of events—due, if nothing else, to the existential threat it poses to our hard-won freedoms and rights. As Greenwald says, "denial of right carries costs, and we should not deprive core rights or radically restructure society (both of which carry high costs) in order to avert low risks."

Passport to Tyranny

In January 2021, as vaccine rollouts were beginning in many countries, former British Prime Minister Tony Blair, one of the biggest proponents of vaccine passports—whose foundation, the Tony Blair Institute for Global Change, has received millions of pounds in donations from provaccine organizations such as the Bill and Melinda Gates Foundation—made one of the most Orwellian statements of the pandemic so far. "In the end," Blair said in an interview with ITV news, "vaccination is going to be your route to liberty." This statement could not be further from the truth: vaccination against COVID-19, together with the digital vaccine certificates that accompany it, is a surefire route to tyranny.[2]

Once consolidated, vaccine passport systems will form the foundation of sweeping digital control and surveillance platforms, to which our entire lives could end up being tied. As I will show later on in this book, vaccine passports and digital IDs have been in the planning for years. Some of the tech companies developing the systems are already gushing at the potential business opportunities.[3]

To complement its Green Pass, the EU has launched a digital wallet that will store peoples' surnames, first names, dates and place of birth, gender, and nationality—and enable Europeans to identify themselves online.[4] It is also pushing ahead with its European

Payments Initiative (EPI), whose purpose, as its name implies, is to build and deploy the infrastructure to develop and deliver a pan-European digital payment solution.[5] At the same time, the upcoming launch of central bank digital currencies will enable far greater control over our personal (and, some would say, private) spending habits. All of this could be tied to the vaccine passport systems.[6]

In addition to your identity, something else that won't belong to you anymore once you have a vaccine passport is the power to decide what new, experimental (meaning: largely untested) therapeutics go into your body. This fundamental right is now being systematically ignored by governments, courts, and public health authorities around the world.

One could understand the need for such drastic measures if we were dealing with a virus like smallpox, with a case fatality rate of around 30 percent, or if we were using vaccines that actually prevented contraction of the virus or its spread. But we aren't. These vaccines do not confer sterilizing immunity, and whatever protection they do offer against infection is short-lived. What's more, public health authorities' blind obsession with vaccination comes at the expense of all other interventions, such as early treatment, preventive health, and better ventilation. Even formerly widely used measures including regular testing are now taking a back seat to vaccines in countries such as France and Italy.

Even more worrisome, governments are constantly changing the requirements to qualify for the vaccine passport. The government of Israel, the first country to launch a vaccine passport nationwide, told its citizens in late February 2021 that if they took two jabs of the Pfizer vaccine, two weeks later they would automatically qualify for the so-called Green Pass and all the privileges it confers, such as access to bars, restaurants, university, and other public spaces. But in September the government reneged. After the effects of Pfizer's leaky vaccine began to wane over the summer, Tel Aviv announced that to remain eligible for the Green Pass, Israeli citizens would need to take a booster shot five months after the second dose; otherwise, their Green Pass would be deactivated.[7] At the beginning of 2022, the country began offering a fourth booster to people over 60 and medics, yet cases were once again soaring.[8] Many other governments have since followed suit, with some also requiring a fourth booster.

Just think: One minute, you're a legal citizen able to participate in society, earn an income, and enjoy access to the experiences and services that a legal citizen has access to. The next minute, you're banished to the margins, unable to eke out a living, treated as a non-person, because the government has changed the rules. It is a system designed to force total compliance from a fearful, powerless public.

And human beings are if anything highly malleable and adaptive creatures. If history has taught us anything, it is that we can adapt to just about any situation, including one of brutal, suffocating tyranny. Our minds can make it seem normal. This has happened countless times throughout history and around the world. In just the past century, totalitarian regimes have come and gone, leaving a trail of death, misery, and destruction in their wake. But one thing those regimes didn't have at their disposal, thankfully, is the tracking, surveillance, and control capabilities offered by today's digital IT technologies.

We have already seen more than enough to form an idea of what it will be like to live under the shadow of a vaccine passport system. The European Union's Green Pass System went live on June 1, 2021, ostensibly to control travel between EU nations. By September 1, just three months later, over a dozen of the bloc's 27 Member States were requiring hospitality Green Passes or similar health passports to enter restaurants, bars, museums, gyms, libraries, and other public places.

A License to Live

The Green Pass is not a passport; it is a license to live. For example, Italy, led by current prime minister and former central banker Mario Draghi, who has never been elected to public office in his life, upped the ante on September 17, 2021, by becoming the first major economy in Europe to mandate that all workers, both from the public and private sector, must show their Green Pass to continue in their jobs.[9]

In the United States, things are taking a somewhat different course. In early September of 2021, President Joe Biden reneged on a previous pledge to never issue a vaccine mandate by imposing draconian new vaccine rules on federal workers, large employers, and health care staff. The new requirements could apply to as many as 100 million people—the equivalent of two thirds of the US workforce.

However, the strength of opposition to the Biden administration's vaccine mandates is huge, particularly in Republican-controlled states. In September of 2021 two dozen Republican state attorneys general sent a letter to Biden urging the president to reconsider his decision to mandate vaccinations, calling the plan "disastrous and counterproductive."[10] Within weeks of the mandates coming into effect, most of them had been blocked by court injunctions. By the end of 2021 numerous groups, including business associations and Republican-led states, had asked the Supreme Court to rule on the matter.[11] And that is probably where the final decision about the mandates' legality will be made.

There are also growing signs of resistance on the ground, even in many Democrat-controlled states. In New York, one of the first states to launch a digital vaccine certificate—the so-called Excelsior Pass— local residents, including many municipal workers, have taken their anger against the new restrictions onto the streets a number of times.[12]

The UK has also seen large-scale protests against lockdowns and vaccines passports, which have only intensified after the Boris Johnson government introduced vaccine passports for England in mid-December. But it is the European mainland that saw the biggest protests in 2021—hardly surprising given the EU's central role in pushing vaccine passports. By the end of the year, as the European Commission contemplated making vaccination mandatory across all 27 of its Member States, a huge protest movement was sweeping the continent.

Why the Urgency?

There is still a small but rapidly closing window of time to stop this train wreck from happening. Ultimately, it will depend on the scale and intensity of public opposition.

In September, Spain's Supreme Court ruled against the use of COVID-19 passports altogether as a means of restricting access to public spaces, only to overturn its own ruling a month later.[13] A court in the Wallonia region of Belgium has also ruled that vaccine passports are illegal and may even contravene citizens' rights to data privacy.

While these moves may offer a sliver of hope, time is a luxury we do not have. The speed of change in the pandemic-era world is blistering. At the beginning of 2021, concerns about vaccine passports were dismissed as off-the-wall conspiracy theories. By the end of the year they were being rolled out at a lightning-fast pace across Europe, North America, and even parts of Asia and Latin America. We're being told by governments, public health authorities, scientists, billionaires, vaccine makers, and legacy media that they are the only way of vanquishing the virus and regaining our freedoms. This is a lie, of course, as I will lay out in chapter 1 of this book.

In the meantime, all of the technological inputs needed to create the interlocking systems of digital control, tracking, and surveillance that will usher in the hyper-authoritarian "new normality" already exist. They just need to be put in place, which is exactly what is happening right now. As UK Prime Minister Boris Johnson said in a speech given to the UN General Assembly on September 24, 2019, just months before the pandemic began, "Digital authoritarianism is not the stuff of dystopian fantasy but of an emerging reality."[14]

On the bright side, the official narrative is unraveling in many countries, whether on the lauded benefits of the vaccines, the necessity for booster shots, or the dangers of using cheap, repurposed treatments. Trust in government is plunging as public health authorities keep shifting the goalposts of their policy agenda. For many parents, giving healthy children vaccines that have no long-term safety data for a virus that poses a limited threat to children represents a clear red line, especially when the government's own advisors warn against it, as recently happened in the UK.[15]

There is a risk, however, that as the lies, broken promises, and outright fraud become increasingly apparent to more and more people, governments will resort increasingly to coercion and brute force, as we're already seeing in countries such as France, Germany, and Australia. As George Orwell once wrote, "all tyrannies rule through fraud and force, but once the fraud is exposed they must rely exclusively on force."

Most of us who live in liberal democracies in North America, Western Europe, Japan, or Australasia and were born in the postwar era have little or no experience of what life is like under the thumb of an authoritarian regime—for which we should be eternally grateful. But it also means that we are dangerously complacent. We don't know what it's like to be designated a nonperson by an overweening State and deprived access to basic services, public spaces, or the ability to earn a living. If we are not careful, if we do not treat the threat in front of us seriously enough and take strong, concerted action in the small window of time still available to us, we will soon find out.

CHAPTER ONE

Logical Insanity

VACCINE PASSPORTS ARE A NORMAL, justifiable, and proportionate response to the threat posed by the COVID-19 pandemic. Or so we are told. The passports are no different from other mandated health and safety requirements, such as seat belts or laws that prevent people from smoking on airplanes. Or so we are told. They merely represent upgraded digitized versions of paper vaccine certificates that have been around for a long time. Or so we are told.

None of these claims are true, but they give the comforting impression that nothing much will change as the passports are rolled out and come into effect. Nothing, in fact, could be further *from* the truth.

But the biggest lie of all is that vaccine passports are a small, collective sacrifice that will allow us to return to normality. By "nudging" almost everyone who can get vaccinated to do so, the passports will supposedly help us finally achieve herd immunity and thereby eliminate the virus. And once everyone is vaccinated and poses no contagion risk, we will safely be able to resume normal activities. This line of reasoning is exemplified in an article published by the Australian website *The Conversation*, titled "Vaccine Passports: Why They Are Good for Society": "[V]accine passports are a minimal cost for returning to normal daily life and for reducing anxiety for those you come into contact with on airplanes or in theatres, restaurants, or public stadiums. They are a small sacrifice for a greater good."[1]

This logic is simple but dangerously flawed.

Appealing to the greater good can be an effective—and sometimes necessary—means of securing approval for public measures that involve some degree of individual or collective sacrifice. Few people want to be seen as outliers, especially if it means feeling responsible or being blamed for the suffering and deaths of others.

But there is a fundamental flaw in applying the "greater good" argument to vaccine passports, because the passports themselves—unlike the vaccine certificates of old—offer precious little in the way of potential good and a huge amount in the way of potential harm.

A Brief History

The practice of requiring proof of immunization to access certain spaces or traverse certain borders dates back more than 200 years to Edward Jenner's creation of the smallpox vaccine in 1796. Smallpox had been a major scourge throughout the eighteenth century, killing an estimated 400,000 Europeans each year, including five reigning European monarchs. Around 30 percent—almost one in three—of the people infected with smallpox died from the disease. After Jenner's development of the vaccine, more and more jurisdictions began requesting that travelers present proof of inoculation. The policy was implemented more widely across the globe as international travel grew in the nineteenth century.

This trend intensified after the introduction of air travel in the twentieth century, says Sanjoy Bhattacharya, professor of history at the University of York. Vaccine certification checks were enforced before travel "with forcible isolation at airports of any passengers considered to have dubious documentation."[2] The International Health Regulations (IHR), adopted in 1969, allowed signatory states to demand proof of vaccination as a condition of entry. Today the only disease specified in the IHR is yellow fever, although the World Health Organization (WHO) has urged certain high-risk countries to propose vaccination certificates for diseases that are still prevalent within their borders and to which their population has not been sufficiently inoculated.

The implementation—and imposition—of vaccine passports for COVID-19 is supposed to represent a mere continuation of this long-standing practice. In reality, it represents a sharp deviation. Digital vaccine passports are poles apart from the paper vaccine certificates that have been used over the past two centuries for endemic viruses such as smallpox, polio, and yellow fever. Whereas vaccine certificates have been specifically used to establish vaccine status at certain national borders, today's vaccine passports will have a far broader scope of application. They can be—and in some cases already are—required to travel within one's own country of residence, as well as access basic services or even make a living.

The dichotomy could not be starker. In the first case, failure to provide proof of vaccination meant you could not visit a particular country where vaccination is required. This represented a limited infringement of personal liberty. In the second, failure to provide proof of COVID-19 vaccination could lead to ostracism from society and the total loss of one's basic rights and freedoms.

The stakes could not be higher. If you do not have a vaccine passport, you will be prevented from accessing basic services, from earning a living, or traveling within your own country. Even if you *do* have one, you will be exposed to unprecedented levels of government and corporate surveillance, data mining, and behavioral control. You will no longer have a say over what goes inside your body. Just about everything you do, from boarding a plane, to enrolling your child in a school, to entering a supermarket, will require the consent of government agencies. And that consent can be withdrawn at any moment. Put simply, this is not a return to normality; it is the creation of a starkly different form of existence in which most of us will have virtually no agency over our own lives.

Of course, the new vaccines themselves are very different from the vaccines of old. Vaccines have traditionally taken between 5 and 10 years to develop and fully test. The current crop of COVID-19 vaccines, based on novel technologies, were developed, tested, and rolled out in less than a year. It was a remarkable scientific achievement, but the results have not lived up to expectations. Unlike traditional vaccines, they do not use a killed or attenuated form of the disease to trigger an immune reaction but instead employ a genetic intervention more accurately described as "gene therapy." The immune response they stimulate is much more narrowly focused than that of traditional vaccines and thus easier for the virus to evade.

What's more, the attendant health risks of the COVID-19 vaccines, particularly over the long term, are still not fully understood, as the UK's Joint Committee on Vaccination and Immunisation noted in its recommendation not to jab 12- to 15-year-olds—a recommendation the UK government ignored.[3] Many of the scientific studies used to justify granting the vaccines "emergency use authorization" still haven't been released to the public or even made available to scientists or doctors. According to the WHO, just 12 percent of 86 clinical trials for 20 COVID-19 vaccines have been made publicly available.[4]

The United States Food and Drug Administration (FDA) in November 2021 responded to a freedom of information act (FOIA) request to hand over all of its records pertaining to the COVID-19 vaccines—totaling some 330,000 pages—by proposing to release just 500 pages per month on a rolling basis. In other words, the US public—and by extension, the global public—will not know what the FDA currently knows about the safety and efficacy of the COVID-19 vaccines until 2097, by which point many of us will already have died. Even the Reuters news agency, whose CEO sits on the board of vaccine maker Pfizer, seemed shocked by the move, publishing a report titled "Wait What? FDA Wants 55 Years to Process FOIA Request over Vaccine Data."[5] In early January, a federal judge in Texas ordered the FDA to release all the data in eight months at a rate of over 55,000 pages a month. As Reuters reported, "that's roughly 75 years and four months faster than the FDA said it could take to complete the Freedom of Information Act request."[6]

Most significantly, traditional vaccines prevent infection and transmission. The COVID-19 vaccines do not.[7] A traveler required to take, say, a yellow fever vaccine can rest assured that the vaccine is not only extremely safe but will also provide near-total protection from catching the virus—not only for the duration of the visit but for many years after. And host country authorities can also be confident that the traveler will not become a vector of contagion during his or her journey.

The same cannot be said of the COVID-19 vaccines. They do not confer strong, lasting immunity from infection or transmission of the virus. As even the CDC admitted, both vaccinated and unvaccinated infected people are infectious to others. A CDC study leaked to the *New York Times* showed that viral loads are similar for both vaccinated and unvaccinated people.[8] In addition, whatever protection against transmission and infection the vaccines do offer against the Delta variant wanes quickly. Against Omicron, the protection is even weaker and shorter lasting.

The Illusion of Immunity

By mid-2021 hopes were still high that if enough people were vaccinated, countries would achieve herd immunity. This is despite the fact that the vaccines never promised to offer sterilizing immunity, in which the immunity is so complete that the virus can't gain a foothold in a vaccinated individual. But that didn't stop public health authorities and other government agencies from propagating the idea. In May 2021, the director of the US National Institute of Allergy and Infectious Diseases and President Biden's chief medical advisor, Dr. Anthony Fauci, said the more people who get vaccinated, the more we approach eliminating the virus instead of merely controlling it. "And that's the reason why we continue to push to get those people who are reluctant to get vaccinated, to, in fact, get vaccinated."

But then the Delta variant arrived and upended expectations. By July 2021, COVID-19 cases, hospital admissions, and deaths were soaring across the United States. Vaccine advocates were quick to blame the new wave of infections on the populace's failure to hit the government's benchmarks. The Biden administration even called the summer outbreak a "pandemic of the unvaccinated" and admonished the vaccine-hesitant with language such as "we've been patient but our patience is wearing thin," a grave mistake for at least two reasons: First, it stigmatized the unvaccinated, further aggravating tensions in an already divided country; and second, it offered people who were vaccinated a false sense of security that they were protected from infection.[9]

Beyond US shores, in countries where health authorities were tracking breakthrough cases more closely, the evidence against vaccine efficacy was stacking up. Data emerging from Israel, which injected most of its population in January and February of 2021 with the Pfizer vaccines, was showing by June that not only were the vaccines exceptionally leaky against the Delta variant, but the limited protection they did confer waned after only a few months. Another study by Oxford University and reported in the *Financial Times* found that "the efficacy of the Pfizer vaccine against symptomatic infection almost halved after four months, and that vaccinated people infected with the more infectious Delta variant had as high viral loads as the unvaccinated."[10]

This, together with Delta's extreme infectiousness and ability to evade the vaccine's defenses, explains why some of the world's most vaccinated countries, from Iceland to the UK to Singapore, as well as some of the most vaccinated states in the United States, including Vermont, Hawaii, and Oregon, suffered far worse summer outbreaks in 2021 than they had in 2020.

In the UK, 84 percent of people over the age of 12 had received at least one dose and 75 percent had received both as of September 1, 2021.[11] Yet the number of hospitalized patients and patients on ventilators between early June and early September increased roughly ninefold.[12] By mid-September more fully vaccinated people over the age of 40 were catching the virus than the unvaccinated cohort, according to the government's own figures.[13]

On December 8, 2021, the UK government reported that between weeks 45 and 48 of that year—roughly equating to the month of November—fully vaccinated people accounted for 47 percent of the total number of COVID-19 cases in the country (compared to 39 percent for unvaccinated) and 56 percent of COVID-19-related hospital admissions (compared to 39 percent for unvaccinated). If you include people who had received just one dose of a vaccine, the vaccinated cohort accounted for 55 percent of recorded cases during the period and 60 percent of hospital admissions.

It was a similar story in Israel, which saw a 700-fold increase in cases in the space of two and a half months during 2021. At the beginning of June, the country was recording approximately 15 cases a day. Most people were vaccinated and the pandemic was considered as good as over. A month later, by July 1, the number of daily cases had shot up to 290. A month and a half after that, in mid-September, the number of daily cases had reached 11,000. Largely vaccinated Israel was recording over 2,000 more cases than at any other time during the pandemic. By mid-August most hospitalized people were vaccinated; as *Science Magazine* reported:

As of 15 August, 514 Israelis were hospitalized with severe or critical COVID-19, a 31% increase from just 4 days earlier. Of the 514, 59% were fully vaccinated. Of the vaccinated, 87% were 60 or older. 'There are so many breakthrough infections that they dominate and most of the hospitalized patients are actually vaccinated,' says Uri Shalit, a bioinformatician at the Israel Institute of Technology (Technion) who has consulted on COVID-19 for the government. One of the big stories from Israel [is]: 'Vaccines work, but not well enough.'[14]

By this point, it was clear that so-called "breakthrough cases" were not as rare as their name suggests. Centers for Disease Control (CDC) Director Rochelle Walensky admitted that the messenger RNA (mRNA) vaccines do not prevent COVID-19 infection, nor do they stop the vaccinated person from transmitting the infection, although she emphasized that the vaccine still provides strong protection against hospitalization or death.[15]

In September 2021, S. V. Subramanian, a Harvard professor of population health and geography, published a paper in the *European Journal of Epidemiology* that found that "increases in COVID-19 were unrelated to levels of vaccination across 68 countries and 2,947 US counties." Subramanian concluded his paper by asserting that although vaccines significantly reduce the risk of hospitalization and death from COVID-19, the "sole reliance on vaccination as a primary strategy to mitigate COVID-19 and its adverse consequences needs to be re-examined . . . other pharmacological and non-pharmacological interventions may need to be put in place alongside increasing vaccination."[16]

In the UK, Sir Andrew Pollard, the director of Oxford Vaccine Group, cautioned that, since the emergence of the Delta variant, "herd immunity is not a possibility" with the current crop of vaccines, as the virus "still infects vaccinated individuals."

He added, "And I suspect that what the virus throws up next is a variant that is perhaps even better at transmitting within vaccinated populations."[17] Which is exactly what happened.

In October 2021, a highly contagious COVID-19 variant with unusually high numbers of mutations on the spike protein gained a foothold in South Africa. Thanks to those mutations, it almost completely evaded the current crop of vaccines. According to preliminary analyses, the Pfizer vaccine provided just 33 percent protection against infection, compared to 80 percent protection before the new variant's emergence.[18] The Moderna vaccine fared little better. Other vaccines offer even less protection against infection and transmission of the new variant, reported the *New York Times* on December 19.[19]

Dubbed Omicron, the variant spread like wildfire across the globe. By the beginning of 2022, it was the dominant variant in many countries and super spreader events involving largely vaccinated people were taking place all over the world. Many countries in Europe, the world's most vaccinated continent, were registering record levels of cases and some countries, including Denmark, Greece, and Italy, were reimposing testing requirements for all travelers, including EU nationals, regardless of their vaccination status. Israel, the most "boostered" country on planet Earth, was in the grip of its fifth wave of infections.

All of which begs the question: If a vaccinated person still has a marked propensity to carry, shed, and transmit the virus, particularly in its Delta or Omicron variant forms, what difference does a vaccination passport, certificate, or ID make in preventing spread of the virus?

Public Health Madness

As conditions have changed, so, too, has the narrative around the vaccines. Now, the focus is squarely on the protection they confer against hospitalization and death. But one thing that hasn't changed is the policy response of public health agencies. Governments around the world are still plowing ahead with plans to impose vaccine passports and mandates on their respective populations. In countries such as the

United States and Australia, senior policymakers, including US President Joe Biden, continued to blame the unvaccinated for the spread of the virus. In the fall of 2021, Dr. Fauci insisted that "many, many more mandates" will be needed to bring the pandemic under control.[20]

Dr. Fauci argued that everyone should be prepared (or if necessary compelled) to "give up their individual right of making" their "own decision for the greater good of society":

> [A]s a member of society reaping all the benefits of being a member of society, you have a responsibility to society. And I think each of us, particularly in the context of a pandemic that's killing millions of people, you have got to look at it and say, there comes a time when you do have to give up what you consider your individual right. Of making your own decision for the greater good of society. There's no doubt that that's the case.[21]

Dr Fauci said these words in late October 2021, by which time it was clear the Delta variant was evading the vaccines with disconcerting ease. Multiple studies from countries such as Vietnam, the UK, and the United States had shown that infected vaccinated people were carrying very similar levels of virus in their upper respiratory tracts as infected unvaccinated people. Then came the hyper-contagious Omicron variant, which has proven to be even more adept at evading not only the vaccines but also infection-acquired immunity.

"A number of studies are converging on the fact that 2 doses of vaccination has poor vaccine effectiveness against Omicron," wrote US hematologist-oncologist and health researcher Vinay Prasad on January 9 in his blogpost "Vaccine Effectiveness (Against Infection Not Severe Disease) Goes Down the Drain." Prasad added that while three doses fare slightly better, "the effect will rapidly wane as antibody titers fall, and infection is certain as the number of exposures increase."[22]

By early January 2022—just over a year after the vaccine rollouts began—many of the world's most vaccinated countries were registering record numbers of cases. In heavily vaccinated Italy, Spain, and Portugal the infection curve was so high that it dwarfed all previous waves. All eyes were on Israel, the first country to mandate booster shots for its population. On January 12, the number of new daily infections hit 41,154, shattering all previous records.

Clearly, Fauci's claim that each individual has a responsibility to be vaccinated to limit spread of the virus to others does not pass master in the Omicron era. The decision to be vaccinated has become almost entirely personal, says Prasad:

> *This is not an argument about the benefits of vaccination for the individual—vaccines likely (and evidence shows they) still have great protection against severe disease; instead, this is an argument about the effects of vaccination on symptomatic disease and (some good portion of) transmission. Conclusion: you cannot contain the viral spread of omicron by boosting.* [23]

What's more, it is by now more or less clear that immunity from previous infection provides broader and longer-lasting protection against the virus than vaccine-induced immunity. This is not to say that people should intentionally infect themselves (and risk suffering severe symptoms) or that public health authorities should seek to achieve herd immunity but rather that public health policy should at least recognize that natural immunity confers superior protection against future infection. In August 2021 a real-world observational study conducted in Israel examined the medical records of tens of thousands of Israelis, tracking their infections, symptoms, and hospitalizations between June 1 and August 14.[24] What the study found was that never-infected people who were vaccinated in January and February were 6 to 13 times more likely to get infected four to six months down the line than unvaccinated people who were previously infected with the coronavirus.

Many other studies have since confirmed this trend, though there has been one key outlier. A CDC study based on data on 7,000 people across nine states and 187 hospitals claims that people hospitalized with "coronavirus-like" symptoms (a term that should already set off alarm bells) are over five times more likely to test positive for COVID-19 if they had had recent prior infection than if they were recently vaccinated.

Besides the use of the ambiguous term "COVID-like symptoms," there are other reasons to question the validity of the trial. First, the CDC has an explicit policy of pressuring people who have already had a COVID-19 infection to get vaccinated as quickly as possible. Indeed, the conclusion of the study was that "eligible persons should be vaccinated against COVID-19 as soon as possible, including unvaccinated persons previously infected with SARS-CoV-2."[25] In the EU, by contrast, people who can prove they have had an infection are considered immune, albeit only for six months. Swiss authorities recently bumped up the period of presumed immunity as a result of natural infection from six months to a year.[26]

Second, the CDC has done a poor job of tracking breakthrough cases since the vaccine rollouts began, while authorities in Israel and the UK have tracked them meticulously. There is even evidence to suggest that the CDC has been manipulating its vaccination data. As *Kaiser Health News* reported in December 2021, for over a month the CDC had been reporting that 99.9 percent of everyone over the age of 65 had received at least one dose of a COVID-19 vaccine:

> *That would be remarkable—if true.*
>
> *But health experts and state officials say it's certainly not.*
>
> *They note that the CDC as of Dec. 5 has recorded more seniors at least partly vaccinated—55.4 million—than there are people in that age group—54.1 million, according to the latest census data from 2019. The CDC's vaccination rate for residents 65 and older is also significantly higher than the 89% vaccination rate found in a poll conducted in November by KFF [Kaiser Family Foundation].*
>
> *Similarly, a YouGov poll, conducted last month for* The Economist, *found 83% of people 65 and up said they had received at least an initial dose of vaccine.*

And the CDC counts 21 states as having almost all their senior residents at least partly vaccinated (99.9 percent). But several of those states show much lower figures in their vaccine databases, including

California, with 86 percent inoculated, and West Virginia, with nearly 90 percent as of December 6.[27] Another CDC study, published in August, suggested that people who have been vaccinated are 11 times less likely to die of COVID-19 than people who haven't. Again, this has raised the pressure on people to get vaccinated. Yet the results also clash with data coming out of other countries. For example, in the UK, where breakthrough cases have been tracked extremely closely, 75 percent of the patients who died "of" or "with" COVID-19 between weeks 45 and 48 of 2021 had received both shots of one of the vaccines while 21 percent were unvaccinated. Given that just over 80 percent of the UK's population had received both doses of the vaccine by late November, vaccination clearly offers some degree of protection against death from COVID-19 but not nearly as much as the CDC study claims.

For its part, the UK government was at pains to underscore that the data does not in any way undermine the purported efficacy of the COVID-19 vaccines at protecting people from hospitalization or death:

In the context of very high vaccine coverage in the population, even with a highly effective vaccine, it is expected that a large proportion of cases, hospitalisations and deaths would occur in vaccinated individuals, simply because a larger proportion of the population are vaccinated than unvaccinated and no vaccine is 100% effective.[28]

While that is correct, as is the fact that the number of deaths caused by COVID-19 have fallen significantly between March 2021 and January 2022, even as case numbers have surged to a new record, it is also undeniable that the COVID-19 vaccines have proven to be much less effective at containing disease transmission than other vaccines. In October 2021 even Dr. Anthony Fauci, the chief medical advisor to the president and director of the National Institute of Allergy and Infectious Diseases (NIAID), conceded that with the current crop of vaccines, it is "going to be very difficult, at least in the foreseeable future and maybe ever, to truly eliminate this highly transmissible virus."

By now it is clear that vaccinated and unvaccinated people infected with COVID-19 have similar viral loads, that fully vaccinated individuals can catch SARS-CoV-2 as well as spread it to others, sometimes even leading to severe and fatal COVID-19, including among other fully vaccinated individuals.

This is confirmed by a growing body of real-world cases of mass infection among the vaccinated. They included the Boardmasters Festival in the UK in August 2021. To attend the event, music, surfing, and skateboard fans had to provide their NHS Pass, proving a recent negative test, full vaccination, or COVID-19 infection in the past 180 days (the same conditions required by the EU's Green Pass). Yet a week after the event, almost 5,000 COVID-19 cases—approximately 10 percent of all attendees—had been linked to the event.[29] Newquay, the city where it was held, briefly became England's "COVID capital," registering nearly four times the average rate of infection in the country.

The event organizers did everything by the book, yet the result was still a massive spike in infections. Something similar happened at Harvard Business School, which was forced to move its first-year and some second-year MBA students to remote learning after reporting an outbreak of sixty COVID-19 cases within a few weeks of reopening for the fall semester. This despite the fact that 95 percent of students and 96 percent of faculty had been vaccinated against COVID-19.[30]

In July of 2021, two residents of a small, rural South Dakota nursing home died of COVID-19 and others fell ill, even though 100 percent of the care home's elderly residents were fully vaccinated. "The outbreak in the Good Samaritan Society–Deuel County senior care facility in Clear Lake, South Dakota, mirrors a rise in vaccine breakthroughs in nursing homes across the nation," reported the local newspaper *Grand Forks Herald*.[31]

During the same month around 100 cases of COVID-19 were reported on board the Royal Navy's flagship, HMS *Queen Elizabeth*. Several other warships in the fleet accompanying it were also affected, reported the BBC. According to the UK's Defense Secretary Ben Wallace, all crew on the deployment had received two doses of a COVID-19 vaccine.[32]

In the Spanish city of Malaga, 68 nurses and medics working in the intensive care unit at a hospital tested positive for COVID-19 in early December after attending a Christmas party. All of them had had the third booster jab or antigen tests before attending the party, according to Spanish health authorities.

In Lithuania, the first EU member to enforce a society-wide COVID Pass, cases soared so dramatically following implementation that hospitals were forced to turn away nonurgent patients.[33] It is a similar story across the EU. By late November 2021, five months after the introduction of the Green Pass, Europe was once again the epicenter of the COVID-19 pandemic. In the two months after Rome took the drastic step in mid-October of banning all unvaccinated Italians from working within the formal economy, the number of daily cases surged around fivefold. In France, one of the first countries to ban people without the vaccine passport from accessing all hospitality venues, case numbers were once again setting a record high by mid-November.

These fast-multiplying real-world cases should be enough to bring vaccine passport rollouts to a grinding halt, or at the very least slow them down. Not only do these measures fail to prevent or even dramatically reduce the spread of the virus; they may, as evidenced in Lithuania, worsen public health outcomes. Yet governments around the world continue to intensify their efforts to force vaccine passports onto their populations. That makes no sense, at least not from a public health perspective.

A Shockingly Bad Deal

If vaccine passports don't improve public health, why are the governments of the world's most advanced economies going to such lengths to roll them out?

Because vaccine passports offer an unprecedented degree of control over a population. The powerful digital tech platforms offer a highly efficient means to identify, locate, segregate, coerce, and punish those who refuse to submit by stripping them of their jobs, banning them from school, barring them from travel (even within their own country), and even denying them medical treatment or access to food.

But it's not just about control; it's also about money. Large companies in the tech, financial, and pharmaceutical industries stand to reap huge dividends from the new economy taking shape around us. The COVID vaccines have already spawned nine new billionaires in the pharmaceutical industry. There will no doubt be more. Pfizer expected to sell $33-billion-worth of its COVID-19 vaccine in 2021.[34] That would make it the second-highest revenue-generating drug ever. Thanks to its vaccine, Spikevax, Moderna turned its first ever quarterly profit in 2021.[35] In a sick irony, the quicker the effects of the vaccines wear off, the more money the companies stand to earn, as booster jabs open up the possibility of recurring business income. Vaccine mandates and vaccine passports will help the companies to maximize that income.

All this is playing out in plain sight, before our eyes. Consider this: Among those losing their jobs for refusing the jab are many doctors, nurses, and health care workers who saved thousands of lives and were hailed as heroes during the first waves of the pandemic. Not only is this a poor way to thank them; it denies the possibility that they may be better positioned than almost anyone to assess the risks and benefits of a new medical procedure. In the UK, 111,000 of the National Health Service's 1.32 million workers were still unvaccinated and yet to receive a single dose as of early October, despite a looming vaccine mandate.[36]

Many proponents of vaccine passports and mandates cite as precedent the 1905 Supreme Court case of *Jacobson vs. Massachusetts*, in which the court upheld the authority of states to enforce compulsory vaccination laws, in that case for smallpox. But there are three important differences between *Jacobson vs. Massachusetts* and the mandates and vaccine passports being rolled out for COVID-19. First, the average case fatality rate for acute smallpox infections was a staggering 30 percent; for COVID-19 it's between 1 percent and 2 percent for the general population and lower for people who don't have specific comorbidities. Second, the smallpox vaccine had a 100-year track record; at the time of the Supreme Court's ruling, there was already a great deal of information available about its short- and long-term safety and efficacy, which helped to ensure it enjoyed broad social acceptance. The same cannot be said of the COVID-19 vaccines. Last, and most important, the penalty for noncompliance, which Jacobson was contesting, was a $5 fine. Today, that would be about $155. Jacobson was not threatened with the loss of employment or livelihood. Nor was he threatened with the loss of freedom of movement or the ability to take part in society.

The current vaccine passports and mandates do not represent a proportionate, ethical, or effective response to the threat posed by COVID-19 pandemic, and therefore cannot be justified.

In the UK, almost 2,000 Christian leaders signed a letter to Prime Minister Boris Johnson warning about the existential threat posed by vaccine passports to the country's liberal democracy:

> *We risk creating a two-tier society, a medical apartheid in which an underclass of people who decline vaccination are excluded from significant areas of public life. There is also a legitimate fear that this scheme would be the thin end of the wedge leading to a permanent state of affairs in which COVID vaccine status could be expanded to encompass other forms of medical treatment and perhaps even other criteria beyond that. This scheme has the potential to bring about the end of liberal democracy as we know it and to create a surveillance state in which the government uses technology to control certain aspects of citizens' lives. As such, this constitutes one of the most dangerous policy proposals ever to be made in the history of British politics.[37]*

From the very beginning, we were sold a quick-fix solution: Just take two shots of one of the vaccines (or one in the case of Johnson & Johnson's) and you'll be safe and protected and life can return to normal. What we actually got was something quite different: a trade-off, with pros and cons of gargantuan proportions. Anyone with even a smidgen of business acumen—or who has ever even bought something off Amazon only to be disappointed by the product upon its arrival—will recognize this kind of bait and switch for what it is: a bad deal.

At some point, the world's global citizens—including those who are vaccinated—need to ask ourselves what we stand to gain from vaccine passports. As recent experience in Europe has shown, they will do precious little to stop the spread of a disease that many virologists and epidemiologists are now warning will become endemic, anyway. In return, we are being asked to give up just about everything that matters—or at least should matter: our privacy; control over our own bodies; control over our own lives; basic core freedoms, such as the ability to earn a living, to feed our families, to travel within our own countries, to receive an education, to assemble, to sit at a café and have a drink with our friends on an outdoor terrace. Even if you are fully vaccinated—meaning you are fully up to date with all the booster shots—you will still have to submit to unfettered tech-enabled surveillance, tracking, and control in a two-tiered checkpoint society.

Vaccine passports have been sold to the public as a good deal—something that will allow us to return to our lives. But in fact, they are a shockingly bad deal for almost everyone. We do not have a seat at the negotiating table. Nor have we been consulted on the terms and conditions of the deal—a deal that promises to hand over vast new powers to government agencies and create vast new markets and opportunities in the tech, finance, and pharmaceutical sectors, while stripping individuals of our basic rights and freedoms. And as I will cover in chapter 2, it's a deal that contravenes the most basic national and international human rights laws.

CHAPTER TWO

Your Body, Their Choice

UNTIL THE YEAR 2021 bodily autonomy and integrity were not controversial concepts. They were fundamental human rights, enshrined in national laws and international charters, such as the Nuremberg Code. Created in 1947 with the aim of ensuring the excesses of coerced health care and medical experimentation during the Nazi era would never be repeated, the Nuremberg Code sent a clear message to the world's global citizens: your body is your own from a medical standpoint and it's your choice what medical interventions it is subjected to and what goes inside it.

Its first clause states that "the voluntary consent of the human subject is absolutely essential" for any medical intervention to satisfy moral, ethical, and legal standards:

> *This means that the person involved should have legal capacity to give consent; should be so situated as to be able to exercise free power of choice, without the intervention of any element of force, fraud, deceit, duress, overreaching, or other ulterior form of constraint or coercion; and should have sufficient knowledge and comprehension of the elements of the subject matter involved as to enable him to make an understanding and enlightened decision.* [1]

Bodily autonomy refers to the right to make decisions over one's own life and future. It is about being empowered to make informed choices. Bodily integrity is the right of each human being, including children, to self-ownership and self-determination over their own body. Together, the two principles mean that doctors, scientists, and researchers do not have the right to administer any medical treatment or procedure without the patient's informed consent.

Vaccine mandates and vaccine passports violate both principles, since they seek to compel or coerce people to take an experimental medical product against their will. By doing so, they threaten to cancel the very notion that human beings have agency over their own bodies.

"Not only is bodily autonomy a human right, it is the foundation upon which other human rights are built." These are the words of the United Nations Population Fund (UNFPA), a UN agency whose mission is to improve reproductive and maternal health worldwide. If, as UNFPA claims, the principle of bodily autonomy is the foundation upon which other human rights are built, then taking it away will also have huge implications for those human rights. In its report "My Body Is My Own," published in April 2021, UNFPA underscores the importance of bodily autonomy—specifically in relation to women's decision-making power over their sexual and reproductive health. But many of its statements are couched in general terms (emphasis my own):

> *Bodily autonomy is about the right to make decisions over one's own life and future. It is about being empowered to* make informed choices. These are universal values. *Governments everywhere have committed, in a variety of international agreements, to protecting autonomy.* Respect for autonomy is a core tenet of international medical ethics.

> Your body is yours and yours only. And so are any decisions about your body.

> *Collective decision-making is common across cultures, societies and governments.* But group decisions cannot circumscribe the rights of individuals. [2]

Yet that is exactly what is happening right now in countries all over the world. The decisions of large groups of people—including governments, public health agencies, supranational organizations, and global corporations—are circumscribing the basic rights of individuals who don't want to have a medical product injected into their bodies. The administration of those vaccines—and their accompanying passports—hinge not on the informed consent of the individual but on mandatory adoption, or in many cases coercion (threatening to deny people the ability to earn a living or access basic services is textbook coercion).

The classic counterargument to this is "your rights end where my safety begins." In other words, while people have a right to bodily autonomy, they can enjoy that right as long as they are not threatening the bodily autonomy of others. This is the way the issue has been framed by the legacy media and public health authorities. Because COVID-19 threatens the safety and bodily autonomy of others, there must be limitations to its application that did not pertain to medical experimentation during the Nazi era.

While this is a legitimate argument, it places vaccine mandates and passports among the most important legal and ethical questions that a society can ever grapple with—on a par with issues like abortion, the death penalty, or the right to die. All of which means that vaccine mandates and passports should be under discussion at the Supreme Court, in parliament, and every dinner table in every country in the world—not simply a fait accompli pronouncement that everyone in the world is expected to adhere to without question.

Instead of having that debate, governments are using emergency laws to bulldoze vaccine mandates and passports into force. In the United States there still isn't an official government document, whether in the form of legislation, law, or regulation, that grants a legal basis for President Biden's mandate. In early November 2021, the US Occupational Safety and Health Administration (OSHA) did release its COVID-19 Vaccination and Testing Emergency Temporary Standard (Vaccine and Testing ETS), which would require that companies with 100 employees get regularly tested for COVID-19 or take the vaccine. But within days the US Court of Appeals for the Fifth Circuit had already paused the implementation of the vaccine requirements, which the court described as a "a one-size-fits-all sledgehammer that makes hardly any attempt to account for differences in workplaces (and workers)."[3]

In December 2021, the US Sixth Circuit Court of Appeals in Cincinnati overturned that ruling, meaning that the vaccine-or-test requirement for workers at companies with 100 or more employees could once again take effect. OSHA said the vaccine mandate would come into effect on January 10, 2022, but just days later the United States Supreme Court placed a temporary block on the vaccine-or-test requirement.[4]

A similar tack was taken by the UK government. When it realized the full extent of backbench opposition to its draft vaccine passport legislation, it decided to shelve the proposed legislation. Two days later, it announced what it called "Plan B" contingency measures, which included mandatory vaccine passport rules.

Vaccine Mandates versus Bodily Autonomy

Here is the contradiction: While bodily autonomy is enshrined in international law, vaccine mandates are legal in many jurisdictions. A study published last year in *Vaccine*, an open-access journal published by *Science Direct*, titled "Global Assessment of National Mandatory Vaccination Policies and Consequences of Non-compliance," analyzed this issue in 193 countries. The study found that over half (105) of the countries have some kind of nationwide mandatory vaccination policy in place. Of those, 62 countries imposed one or more penalties for noncompliance, mostly financial or educational (such as refusing school enrollment).[5]

Given the huge threat that infectious diseases can pose to public health, vaccine mandates are, at times, legitimate and justifiable. But they must be proportionate to the threat posed by the virus as well as the efficacy of the vaccines being mandated. As I argued in chapter 1, the penalties for noncompliance with the COVID-19 vaccine mandates are disproportionately punitive, a major ethical violation when you're asking people to forfeit their right to bodily autonomy.

In the United States, vaccine mandates are legal but they have been used sparingly, especially at the federal level. Neither Dwight

Eisenhower nor John F. Kennedy nor Lyndon Johnson ever resorted to threatening US citizens with the loss of their jobs during their administrations' inoculation campaigns against polio and smallpox.

Even President Joe Biden himself said he wouldn't impose a vaccine mandate, before doing just that in September 2021.[6] Rather than relying on persuasion or calls to civic duty, as Eisenhower, Kennedy, and Johnson had before him, he "hectored, demonized, shamed, politicized, and threatened," wrote Charles Lipson, a professor of political science at the University of Chicago. "That has become his routine, along with his refusal to answer the public's pressing questions."[7]

Many of those questions concern long-term vaccine safety. Given the severity of short-term adverse reactions to the COVID-19 vaccines—including menstrual irregularities, Bell's palsy, blood clots, heart attacks, strokes, and sudden death—concerns about long-term health risks are not only reasonable but responsible. In September 2021, two top scientists at the Federal Drug Administration (FDA)—the Director and Deputy Director of the Office of Vaccines Research Marion Gruber and Philip Kause—resigned as the Biden administration sought to fast track the rollout of COVID-19 booster shots. Although neither Gruber nor Kause gave a reason for their departure, they were among 18 vaccine experts who two weeks later signed a letter to the medical journal *Lancet* cautioning about administering boosters too soon or too frequently:

Although the benefits of primary COVID-19 vaccination clearly outweigh the risks, there could be risks if boosters are widely introduced too soon, or too frequently, especially with vaccines that can have immune-mediated side-effects (such as myocarditis, which is more common after the second dose of some mRNA vaccines, or Guillain-Barre syndrome, which has been associated with adenovirus-vectored COVID-19 vaccines). If unnecessary boosting causes significant adverse reactions, there could be implications for vaccine acceptance that go beyond COVID-19 vaccines. Thus, widespread boosting should be undertaken only if there is clear evidence that it is appropriate.[8]

Since the publication of this letter, both the FDA and the US Center for Disease Control (CDC) have authorized booster shots manufactured by Pfizer BioNTech, Moderna, and Johnson & Johnson. This despite growing concerns about the risks the vaccines may pose, especially to teenage boys and young men. As doctors in the United States began administering Moderna's booster jab to people of all ages, health authorities in Sweden indefinitely extended a moratorium on giving the Moderna vaccine to anyone under the age of 31. Finland, Iceland, and Denmark took similar steps while Norway is encouraging males under 30 not to get the shot. In early January 2022, the European Medicines Agency went a step further, cautioning that regular booster shots of any COVID-19 vaccine could undermine the immune response.[9]

Breaking Laws Left, Right, and Center

In October, Italy's government, led by former European Central Bank chairman Mario Draghi, introduced a law that made it impossible for anyone without a vaccine passport to work in the public or private sector. Italy's "no jab, no job" rule applies to workers of all kinds, including the self-employed, domestic staff, and even people working remotely. Unvaccinated workers were given the option of showing proof of a negative test every two days. But that could cost as much as €50 each time—well beyond the means of most workers—and was withdrawn as an option anyway in early December.[10] Any worker who refused to get vaccinated faced unpaid suspension as well as a fine of up to €1,500. At the time of its entry into law, there were 3.8 million unvaccinated workers in Italy—more than one and a half times the total number of those who were officially unemployed.

The Italian government's new legislation is a mandate in all but name. Workers must submit to receiving a vaccine against their will or face unemployment. As the Italian journalist Thomas Fazi pointed out, this kind of discrimination is in direct violation of the EU's own regulations on vaccine passports (2021/953), which states that "[t]he issuance of [COVID-19] certificates . . . should not lead to discrimination on the basis of the possession of a specific category of certificate," and that "[i]t is necessary to prevent direct or indirect discrimination against persons who are not vaccinated, for example because of medical reasons . . . or because they have not yet had the opportunity or chose not to be vaccinated."[11]

Italy's "no jab, no job" rule also contravenes the Nuremberg Code, which while not officially accepted as law in any country, is widely considered to be the most important document in the history of clinical research ethics.[12] The Code was specifically drafted to address medical experimentation but has since served as a blueprint for many of today's legal and ethical standards, including the Helsinki Declaration of 1964, which in turn has been codified in national or regional legislation and regulations. The Declaration built on the 10 principles first stated in the Nuremberg Code. Crucially, it also tied them to the Declaration of Geneva (1948), a statement of physicians' general ethical duties.[13] Those statements include the following: "I WILL RESPECT the autonomy and dignity of my patient."

The rule also violates the EU's Charter of Fundamental Rights, which holds that "everyone has the right to respect for his or her physical and mental integrity. In the fields of medicine and biology, the following must be respected in particular: the free and informed consent of the person concerned, according to the procedures laid down by law."[14]

Both the Nuremberg Code and the EU's Charter of Fundamental Rights are in agreement: forcing medical procedures upon someone who doesn't want them contravenes an individual's basic right to bodily autonomy and integrity. This violation is particularly flagrant and unjustifiable in the case of a vaccine that was authorized, in the case of the EU, only on a fast-track basis, meaning that the vaccine manufacturers are protected from legal liability for any harm they may cause, or a vaccine that does not confer immunity.

Don't take my word for it, though. That was the conclusion of Switzerland's National Advisory Commission on Biomedical Ethics. In a public statement issued in February 2021, the Commission said that unequal treatment of vaccinated and nonvaccinated people via a vaccination certificate could only be justified if the vaccination in question guaranteed protection against virus. It also averred that a general vaccination obligation in Switzerland would interfere "disproportionately with fundamental rights," and that mandatory vaccination for certain groups of the population, such as health care workers, should be avoided.[15]

Public health authorities should instead focus on making vaccines available to everyone who wants to take one, the Commission said. For those who don't, alternatives such as regular, rapid testing should be made available. The Commission also warned of the broader societal and economic harms the vaccine mandates and passports could cause, such as exacerbating the current shortages of skilled workers—precisely what's happening in many countries, including Italy, France, the UK, and the United States.

Unfortunately, most governments—including Switzerland's—have ignored these recommendations. At the end of November 2021, a clear majority of 62 percent voted in a referendum to keep the government's COVID-19 laws in place, including the vaccine passport.

One result of all this is that millions of frontline workers all over the world who were hailed as heroes in 2020 are now losing their jobs due to their refusal to get vaccinated. They include countless thousands of doctors, nurses, and care workers whom our governments lionized for putting themselves in harm's way, often with inadequate protective equipment, to treat COVID-19 patients in the first waves of the pandemic.

These workers know better than anyone the damage COVID-19 can cause yet they still refuse to get vaccinated. The *Wall Street Journal* reports that some believe the vaccines were rolled out too quickly and are concerned about the possible long-term adverse effects on their health.[16] Some may have already seen first-hand the short-term harm the vaccines can cause. Many of them already have natural immunity from the virus, which more and more studies show is broader and longer lasting then the immunity provided by the vaccines.[17] Yet most vaccine mandates do not exempt those who have already had a SARS-CoV-2 infection. Now many nurses, doctors, and other health care workers face dismissal for exercising their right to bodily autonomy. And health care systems around the world face even worse staff shortages than during the early waves of COVID-19.

Zero Tolerance

For some governments, stripping workers of their ability to work does not go far enough. In Canada the Employment Minister Carla Qualtrough said that those fired for refusing the vaccine should not receive employment insurance (EI). In other words, not only will they lose their livelihood but also all access to other forms of income, including the employment insurance they have contributed to over the course of their working lives.

"It's a condition of employment that hasn't been met," Qualtrough said in an interview with *CBC's Power & Politics*. "And the employer choosing to terminate someone for that reason would make that person ineligible for EI. I can tell you that's the advice I'm getting, and that's the advice I'll move forward with."[18]

Qualtrough's comments elicited a sharp rebuke from some legal experts. Paul Champ, an employment lawyer in Ottawa, told CBC:

I think it's very arguable about whether employees terminated for not getting the vaccine requirement is just cause for termination. I think it's reasonable that some employers may and will terminate employees for not being vaccinated—I don't take issue with that—but it's different to say that it's just cause, meaning you pay them nothing.

To suggest an employer can order an employee to be vaccinated is pushing it, Champ says: "That interferes with bodily integrity and at least my opinion—and I think the consensus among most employment lawyers right now—is that it's not just cause for an employee to refuse that, at least in most circumstances."

Nicholas Wansbutter, a Canadian criminal defense lawyer, believes that the vaccine passports being rolled out by the Trudeau government are not only an affront to a free and democratic society but are also a clear assault on patients' rights:

Medical treatment is an assault if it is not done with not only the consent but the informed consent of a patient. Consent given under fear or duress is ineffective. Consent given under fear or duress is not consent.

> *The implementation of a vaccine passport is absolutely the*
> *exercise of authority. If a person receives a vaccine only because of*
> *that use of authority, and because they want to be able to live a*
> *normal life, they did not consent to medical treatment, and in my*
> *view that is a clear assault. And it is an assault that any physician*
> *is a party to that takes part in. The Hippocratic Oath requires*
> *that physicians do no harm. Assault is harm. A vaccine passport*
> *is absolutely offensive to a free and democratic society.* [19]

In the United States and Canada, universities have even begun to
fire or suspend professors of ethics and bioethics—the very people
who should be helping us to navigate the thorny ethical issues thrown
up by advances in biology, medicines, and technology—for questioning or refusing to comply with their employer's vaccine mandates.
Those professors include University of California Irvine's director of
medical ethics, Dr. Aaron Kheriaty, who was placed on "investigatory
leave" after he challenged the constitutionality of UCI's vaccine mandate in regard to individuals who have recovered from COVID-19
and therefore have naturally acquired immunity. UCI has banned
him from working on campus or working from home.

In a blog post, Kheriaty writes: "How can I continue to call myself
a medical ethicist if I fail to do what I am convinced is morally right
under pressure?" [20]

Dr. Julie Ponesse, an ethicist at Huron University College in
Ontario, lost her job for refusing to abide by her employer's vaccine
mandate and made headlines after filming a tear-filled statement:

> . . . *My employer just mandated that I must get a vaccine for*
> *COVID-19. If I want to keep working in my job as a professor,*
> *I have to take this vaccine. Here's my conundrum: my school*
> *employs me to be an authority on the subject of objective ethics.*
> *I hold a PhD in ethics, an ancient philosophy. And I'm here to*
> *tell you it's ethically wrong to coerce someone to take a vaccine.*
> *If it happens to you, you don't have to do it. If you don't want a*
> *COVID-19 vaccine, don't take one, end of discussion. It's your*
> *own business.*

But that is not the approach of the University of Western Ontario, which has suddenly required that I be vaccinated immediately or not report for work. So, with the school year beginning in a few days, I'm facing imminent dismissal after 20 years on the job because I will not submit to having an experimental vaccine injected into my body.

My job is to teach students how to think critically, to ask questions that might expose a false argument. Questions like: Says who? Who is the authority giving this order? Should I trust them with control over my body? As a professor, I don't have to watch the news to find out if the COVID vaccines are safe. I read medical journals and I consult my colleagues who are professors of science and medicine. I've learnt from doctors that there are serious questions about how safe these vaccines really are. There are questions about how well they work. Nobody is promising that I won't get COVID or transmit COVID if I get the vaccine.

But ultimately none of that matters to me, because I'm a professor of ethics and I'm a Canadian. I'm entitled to make choices about what does and does not enter my body regardless of my reasons. If I'm allowed back into my university, it is my job to teach my students that this is wrong. I'm hired to teach them that it is ethically wrong to impose an experimental medical procedure as a condition of employment. This is my first and potentially last lesson of the year.[21]

The video ends with the written message: "Dr. Ponesse was dismissed from her position on September 7, 2021."

A Slippery Slope to a Dark Place

One of the most worrying aspects of the vaccine mandates and passports—and one that many vaccinated people are only now beginning to fully appreciate—is their ratcheting effects. The government of Israel, the first country to launch a vaccine passport nationwide, told Israeli citizens in February 2021 that all they needed to do to qualify for the so-called Green Pass and all the privileges it confers was to take two jabs of the Pfizer vaccine. The majority of adults and children over the age of 12 complied. But in September the government reneged on its commitment. After the effects of Pfizer's leaky vaccine began to wane over the summer, Tel Aviv announced that to remain eligible for the Green Pass, Israeli citizens would need to take a booster shot five months after the second dose, otherwise, their Green Pass would be deactivated.

Unlike traditional passports or traditional vaccine certificates, these are living digital documents, meaning they can be activated and *deactivated* at any time. This is what makes them such a dangerous tool, especially in the wrong hands. With the click of a mouse or the stroke of a key, they can be turned off if a user no longer meets the requirements. And governments can change those requirements at any time.

By mid-October 2021, the United States was embarking down the same path as Israel. In a press conference CDC Director Dr. Rochelle Walensky said that booster shots may become mandatory in order for people to be considered fully vaccinated:

We have not yet changed the definition of fully vaccinated. We will continue to look at this. We may need to update our definition of fully vaccinated in the future.

Yet as already mentioned, vaccine experts including two former top FDA scientists have already warned of major risks if booster shots "are widely introduced too soon, or too frequently, especially with vaccines that can have immune-mediated side-effects."

Changing the definition not only puts pressure on people to get a booster; it serves two other nefarious ends. First, it opens the door to even tighter control of citizens. As the British journalist Kit Knightly writes, "forcing people to jump through hoops just to 'get back' rights they once took for granted creates an atmosphere that normalizes state tyranny."[22] Second, it makes it more difficult to ascertain the extent of breakthrough cases. After all, anyone who is double-jabbed but has not received a booster shot will be considered unvaccinated. If infected with COVID-19 before receiving the booster or in the two weeks after receiving the booster, they will not be considered a breakthrough case.

By the end of 2021, this had already begun to happen in the UK. As Omicron raged, pushing the country's COVID-19 case numbers to record highs, Prime Minister Boris Johnson issued a statement claiming that "up to 90 percent of the people in ICU are not boosted." Yet when asked by Kate McCann, a political correspondent for Sky News, to clarify the figure, the prime minister's spokesperson said it was based on anecdotal evidence from "some NHS Trusts."[23]

The lesson from this is clear and urgent. When you give up your basic fundamental rights to bodily autonomy and bodily integrity in return for the promise of government-granted privileges, you are on a slippery slope to a dark place. You no longer have control over what goes into your body; the government does. If you have an adverse reaction to the first, second, or third booster shots and you decide that you don't want to have any more, you will be considered unvaccinated. You will lose your privileges. As we are now seeing, governments do not have to honor the promises or commitments they make. But if you want to maintain your temporary privileges, you will be required to do exactly as you are told.

But as you will learn in the next chapter and chapter 5, all citizens are not affected equally by this. When it comes to the vaccine mandates and vaccine passports, some people are more equal than others.

CHAPTER THREE

Divide and Rule

"IN JUST A FEW MONTHS, the new rules have turned my country into a two-tier society of discrimination and hate. Restriction by restriction, it is shredding the bonds that hold us all together in one society." These are the words of Gluboco Lietuva, a Lithuanian husband and father of two children. Neither he nor his wife is vaccinated. On September 21, 2021, he posted a Twitter feed that went viral. In it he chronicled what life was now like after the Lithuanian government had become one of the first EU members to apply the Green Pass to just about every facet of life. He wanted the rest of the world to know what awaits them. It was a story that virtually no international newspaper was bothering to report.

"Without a Pass, you may not enter any shopping center or large supermarket," wrote Lietuva. "At the entrances, people queue in line to be verified. Guards scan the Pass of each person. If you have a valid Pass, the light flashes green and beeps. Then you may enter. No Pass, no entrance."[1]

Without the Lithuanian government's Orwellian-dubbed "Opportunity Pass," Lithuanians cannot enter a restaurant, café, or bar. They cannot step inside a "non-essential" store. They cannot attend higher education or vocational training programs. They cannot access indoor public events or spaces such as conferences, fitness centers, or hair and nail beauty services.[2]

Lithuania introduced no-holes barred segregation in August 2021, ostensibly to "prevent rising coronavirus cases from overwhelming the health care system and to protect people who cannot get vaccinated."[3] Yet the infection curve continued to rise. By early

November it was higher than at any other time during the pandemic. Yet the restrictions stayed in place.

"In just six weeks, the COVID pass has turned my country into a regime of control and segregation," wrote Lietuva. "This is the new society created in Lithuania, the nation furthest along the path to authoritarianism inevitably facing all countries which impose a COVID Pass regime."

A More Divided Planet

Even before the COVID-19 pandemic upended the global economy, economic inequality and social divisions were rising fast across the globe. The year 2019 was "the year of protest." In its final issue of the year, the *New Yorker* reported that movements had "emerged overnight, out of nowhere, unleashing public fury on a global scale—from Paris and La Paz to Prague and Port-au-Prince, Beirut to Bogota and Berlin, Catalonia to Cairo, and in Hong Kong, Harare, Santiago, Sydney, Seoul, Quito, Jakarta, Tehran, Algiers, Baghdad, Budapest, London, New Delhi, Manila, and even Moscow."[4]

The economic fallout of the coronavirus crisis has turbocharged these inequalities. In 2020, the world's billionaires earned considerably more billions than they had even done before, largely thanks to the unprecedented monetary stimulus unleashed by global central banks. The rich were made whole while hundreds of millions of people lost their livelihoods. Now, the stealth emergence of vaccine passports threaten to take economic inequality to a whole new level, by creating a permanent economic underclass while ushering in new forms of tech-enabled discrimination and segregation.

The prime minister of New Zealand Jacinda Ardern openly admitted that her policies will create two classes of people.[5] "If you are still unvaccinated, not only will you be more at risk of catching COVID-19, but many of the freedoms others enjoy will be out of reach," she said. "No-one wants that to happen but we need to minimise the threat of the virus, which is now mainly spreading amongst unvaccinated people."[6]

Two points in this statement are simply not true. Evidence—as I showed in chapter 1—is stacking up that people who are vaccinated represent a similar contagion threat as those who aren't. According to a study published in *Lancet* in late October, someone who is fully vaccinated against COVID-19 yet catches the virus is equally infectious to members of their household as an infected unvaccinated person. Someone fully vaccinated has a 25 percent probability of catching the virus from an infected household member while an unvaccinated contact has a 38 percent probability.[7]

In other words, according to the *Lancet* study, the vaccine offers limited—and even then quickly waning—protection against catching the virus and virtually no protection whatsoever against spreading it. Yet vaccine mandates and passports, in fact, facilitate disease transmission by granting vaccinated people a false sense of security, while subjecting unvaccinated people, including those with natural immunity, to unprecedented restrictions and punishment.

Forgetting the Lessons of History

This is one of the truly dark aspects of the vaccine passport system: It threatens to rip asunder the tenuous threads that keep the social fabric in place. On one side of the divide, a small majority of people—in the case of Lithuania, 58 percent of adults as of early November 2021—are able to continue to more or less go about their daily existence, for the simple reason that they have taken a medical product that doesn't do what it's supposed to. On the other side, a large minority are barred from participating in society at all, for the simple reason that they have decided not to take it.

In the UK, the Equality and Human Rights Commission warned that while the certificates may "in principle" help ease lockdown and travel restrictions, they will do so at the price of creating a "two-tier society whereby only certain groups are able to fully enjoy their rights."[8]

Of course, those so-called "rights" are not rights at all; they are, as Pulitzer Prize-winning journalist Glenn Greenwald put it, "state-granted privileges one earns through compliance with demands of political officials that one inject substances into one's own body." A right is something that is available to all and cannot be rescinded, such as the right to work, raise a family, or practice religion. It also includes freedom of speech and freedom of the press. A privilege, by contrast, can be given and taken away and is considered a special benefit or opportunity available only to certain people.

In an interview on US prime-time news, Dr. Leana Wen, a contributing columnist at the *Washington Post* and medical analyst at CNN, confirmed that through the Biden administration's mandates, the United States was moving toward a system of privileges rather than rights: "We really need to make it clear that there are privileges associated with being an American, that if you wish to have these privileges, you need to get vaccinated."

It's a huge price to pay in return for negligible benefits. As even the UK's Scientific Advisory Group for Emergencies (SAGE) has warned, "vaccine-only certification may only have a very small direct impact on transmission" but at the risk of instituting "potential associated harms and inequalities that should be considered prior to implementation."[9]

Those potential harms include not just excluding people from society or discriminating against them but also scapegoating and dehumanizing them—stripping them of their human qualities, personalities, and dignity. In the United States, public authorities pinned the blame for the summer wave of infections on the unvaccinated, despite growing evidence to the contrary. In Lithuania "principled COVID Pass opposition is caricatured as conspiracy-theorist, antivaxxer," writes Lietuva. "Honest debate is dismissed. Mainstream leaders—politicians, officials, media, the educated elite—openly wish death upon opponents of the Pass 'so we can finally end this pandemic.'"

In Italy, "both Prime Minister Mario Draghi and President Sergio Mattarella have accused unvaccinated people of 'putting the lives of others at risk' (a claim based on the assumption that the vaccinated aren't contagious)," writes Italian journalist and documentary filmmaker Thomas Fazi.[10] Members of the political, medical, and media establishment have also "publicly denounced the unvaccinated for being "rats," "subhumans," and "criminals," who deserve to be "excluded from public life" and "from the national health service," and even to "die like flies."[11]

It is through constant repetition of untruths like these that many national governments have succeeded in promulgating the idea that not being vaccinated means you are a health risk to others while being vaccinated means you are not. In late December, the White House's COVID-19 response coordinator, Jeffrey Zients, told vaccinated people they had "done the right thing and we will get through this." Seconds later, he issued a very different message to the millions of unvaccinated people: "You're looking at a winter of severe illness and death for yourselves, your families, and the hospitals you may soon overwhelm."[12]

The Israeli government's rhetoric, parroted mindlessly by the media, has also grown increasingly threatening, notes journalist and children's author Ziona Greenwald in her blogpost for the *Times of Israel*, "This Is How It Happens":

> *Whether a leader or follower in this race to the bottom it's hard to say, but there's no doubt Israel has lost its moral compass. . . . None of this compares to what took place during the Holocaust. But the galloping evil afoot today could lead to even darker places if it is not called out. When an Israeli TV presenter remarks, "Lockdown the unvaccinated? We ought to put them in cages!" and everybody laughs, we are on dangerous ground. When schoolchildren are put in "cherem" by their classmates because their parents haven't submitted them to a shot, we should all shudder.*
>
> *Unfortunately, most people are in the throes of what satirist-commentator JP Sears describes as a double layer of denial: They're in denial about being in denial. Fellow citizens (be they family members, onetime friends, neighbors, or co-workers) are being stripped of their basic human rights and dignity—not to mention jobs, education, health care, and the benefits due all tax-paying citizens—with the circle of those impacted growing larger as the designation "fully vaccinated" is redefined once*

and again. The bystanders, for now still the majority, reel off well-ingrained justifications and avoid any thoughts that might give rise to compunction. Nothing seems to open their eyes to what's happening.[13]

The ultimate goal is to convince people who are vaccinated that people who are unvaccinated are not only dangerous but unclean, flawed, even subhuman. These include people who are not able to take the vaccine for health reasons such as the chronically ill, those with allergies to one or more of the vaccine components, those who have already suffered a severe reaction to a previous dose of a COVID-19 vaccine, the immune-compromised, children under five, and pregnant or lactating women.

The fact that this is happening in societies that are already deeply stratified, divided, and polarized makes it particularly dangerous. Of course, nobody benefits from the further entrenching of social divisions and animosity other than the political, cultural, and financial elite that are encouraging it.

Words Mark the Start

This process usually begins with language. As noted by the *Philadelphia Inquirer*'s Jeffrey Barg, writing in his "The Grammarian" column, by the summer of 2021 people had begun referring less to "vaccinated people" and more to "the unvaccinated."

That subtle shift from adjective to noun—what nerds call nominalization—affects how vaccinated people view the unvaccinated, and how the unvaccinated view themselves. Its implications are deadly. . . .

[R]eferring to the unvaccinated is a subconscious dehumanization. It's easier for vaccinated people to judge the unvaccinated than vaccine-resistant people. When that language shift happens, walls between the vaccinated and the unvaccinated harden.

But this shift also affects how the so-called unvaccinated view themselves. Referring to the unvaccinated as a group can make them feel, well, like part of a group. Nominalization of the unvaccinated takes a personal choice—the decision not to get a shot—and makes it seem like an innate characteristic. In a desire to be part of this tribe, unvaccinated becomes not just a choice someone made but a definition of who they are.[14]

Unvaccinated people are also reduced to derogatory insults and sound bites: COVIDiots, COVID deniers, conspiracy theorists. Even Queen Elizabeth has taken part, labeling anyone wary of taking an experimental vaccine "selfish." The corporate media is also participating in the name-calling. One *CNN* headline denounced unvaccinated people as "variant factories."[15] An article in *Salon.com* said it is "okay to blame the unvaccinated," since "they are robbing the rest us of our freedoms."[16] This could not be further from the truth: Freedoms are not freedoms if they are capriciously granted and taken away from citizens by the government. An article in *USA Today* encouraged readers to "shun the unvaccinated."[17] American writer Akilah Hughes tweeted to her hundreds of thousands of followers: "Petition to call antivaxxers 'plague rats.'" This not only met with widespread approval but spawned other suggestions, such as "spread necks" and "rat lickers."[18]

This use of offensive, derogatory language serves one main purpose: to dehumanize a subset of the population that has decided, in most cases for legitimate ethical, religious, or health reasons, not to take an experimental gene therapy whose long-term side effects are not yet known. Virtually no effort is made to understand or even discuss the legitimacy of these motivations.

History has taught us—or at least should have by now—that the dehumanization, or "othering," of an entire group of people is never a good thing. Just about every authoritarian system that has existed has, at one time or another, resorted to scapegoating one or several vulnerable minorities, often with horrific consequences. The Soviet Union, particularly during Stalin's reign of terror, targeted the so-called "enemy of the people," a catch-all phrase for anybody deemed not quite Bolshevik enough. Millions ended up perishing in the gulags of Siberia. The Nazis singled out Jewish people, gypsies, those with disabilities, communists, socialists, and other political opponents for systematic persecution and, in many cases, death. But first they stripped them of the essential qualities that made them human in the eyes of others.

In his "Ten Stages of Genocide," Professor Gregory H. Stanton, the founding president of Genocide Watch, a Washington-based NGO, presented a process of steps that lead to a final solution. Stanton placed dehumanization at number 4 in his 10 stages:

> *At this stage, hate propaganda in print, on hate radios, and in social media is used to vilify the victim group. It may even be incorporated into school textbooks. Indoctrination prepares the way for incitement. The majority group is taught to regard the other group as less than human, and even alien to their society. They are indoctrinated to believe that "We are better off without them."*[19]

This is not to say we are on the road to genocide but rather that dehumanizing the countless millions of people who have chosen not to relinquish their bodily autonomy risks setting society down a very dangerous path. As Hannah Arendt argues in her classic book, *The Origins of Totalitarianism*, an overriding impulse of Nazi ideology was to deprive its victims initially of their legal and civil rights and next of their existential rights, ultimately denying perceived enemies of "the right to have rights."

Targeting the Vulnerable

In most countries the people bearing the brunt of the privations are the most vulnerable—the poor, the stateless, migrants, and refugees. They are among the last to receive vaccinations, assuming they are able to get them at all. Even individuals in communities with easy access to the vaccine may not be able to get it due to medical conditions, religious teachings, or restrictions that public health authorities put in place. People on the margins often have less trust in authorities and are less likely to believe government assurances about vaccine safety and efficacy than those in the more closeted classes.

In New York City, one of the first cities in the United States to issue a vaccine passport, more than 70 percent of Black Americans between the ages of 18 and 44 had not taken the vaccine as of late September 2021. As a result, they have been unable to access indoor dining, gyms, museums, theatres, and a host of other indoor activities.

Black Lives Matter activists accused the city's leadership of racism in its vaccine requirements. Hawk Newsome, the cofounder of Black Lives Matter of Greater New York, criticized the city authorities for "excluding a tremendous amount (sic) of Black New Yorkers, from engaging in everyday activities."[20]

What has happened in New York is more or less replicated across state lines. Black and Hispanic people are less likely to have received a vaccine than their Asian or White counterparts. By late October 2021, 70 percent of Asians and 54 percent of Whites had been vaccinated compared to 52 percent of Latinos and 47 percent of Blacks, according to the Kaiser Family Foundation (KFF).[21]

One reason why ethnic minority groups are less willing to take the vaccines is fear of adverse events. Even in mild cases, this can mean having to take one or two days off work. For many low-paid workers, this is not an option. They may lose their jobs, wages, or be demoted. In the case of a more severe adverse event, it could mean costly, and possibly ongoing, medical treatment.

"There's a lot of reasons for [Black people] to mistrust institutions," says Dr. Gary Bennett, a professor of Psychology, Neuroscience, Global Health, and Medicine at Duke University. "Tuskegee looms large in the minds of Black Americans."[22] In the Tuskegee Experiment, which ran from 1932 to 1972, 600 Black men in rural Alabama with syphilis were told they were receiving drugs to treat the disease but were actually given placebos while the researchers studied the effects of untreated syphilis. For 40 years the researchers tracked the course of the untreated disease while promising the research subjects free treatment, until a reporter finally exposed the scandal in 1972. Tuskegee was not the only experiment of its kind. In a trial funded by the US Department of Defense in the 1960s, Dr. Eugene Saenger, an Ohio radiologist credited with advancing medical knowledge on the effects of radiation on the human body, administered dangerously high levels of whole-body radiation to more than 90 poor, Black, uneducated patients with inoperable tumors. As the *LA Times* reported in its 2007 obituary for Saenger, "as many as 20 patients may have died as a result of the radiation and the majority suffered intense pain, persistent nausea, and a variety of other ill effects from the radiation."[23]

Another celebrated American physician, James Marion Sims, conducted research on enslaved Black women. Widely considered the "father of gynecology," the nineteenth-century physician developed a surgical technique to remedy vesicovaginal fistula, a common nineteenth-century complication of childbirth that caused urine leakage and constant pain. But he did so by experimenting on black slaves who could not possibly give their consent to the procedure since they did not own their own bodies. Sims did not even give his subjects anesthesia, since he believed that Black people didn't experience pain as much as White people. Once he had perfected the operation, after four years of experimenting on dozens of subjects, he began performing it on White women, this time using anesthesia.[24]

Then there is the notorious case of Henrietta Lacks, whose story was recently serialized by HBO, based on the award-winning biography *The Immortal Life of Henrietta Lacks*.[25] Lacks was an African American woman who died of cervical cancer in 1951 at the age of 31. During the course of her treatment, scientists at Johns Hopkins realized that her cancer cells reproduced at a much higher rate than most cells, meaning they could be kept alive long enough to allow more thorough examination. This made them hugely valuable for medical research. Those cells, taken without knowledge or consent from Lacks in 1951, became the first, and, for many years, the only human cell line able to reproduce indefinitely and have since been used in research around the world. Neither Lacks nor her family were compensated or benefited in any way.

Medical malfeasance scandals such as these partly explain why Black and Hispanic communities often distrust the medical establishment. But it's not just about lack of trust. Many people have well-thought-out concerns about potential side effects, both short term and long term; the pharmaceutical industry's capture of medicine regulators; the secrecy surrounding the vaccine contracts governments have signed with the vaccine manufacturers; the alleged fraud in Pfizer's vaccine trial; as well as worries about the authoritarianism and loss of civil liberties and privacy that vaccine mandates and passports threaten to unleash.

Instead of acknowledging these concerns as legitimate, many politicians, public health authorities, corporate media, and scientists disparage or patronize those who express them. This, of course, only perpetuates a cycle of distrust.

"Shaming people is bad," says Bennett. "Stigmatizing people will actually lead to the converse of what we expect."

Ironically, many of the people doing the stigmatizing are White so-called "progressives" who speak the language of diversity, equity, and inclusion and profess to hold such values. They claim to care about equality, and yet their legacy, if they are not stopped, may well be the resurrection of racial segregation.

In late November 2021, the medical journal *Lancet* published an article by Dr. Günter Kampf, a widely published researcher at the University of Greifswald in Germany, lambasting public health authorities in both the United States and Europe for promulgating the idea that the unvaccinated are solely to blame for the continued existence of COVID-19 while "people who have been vaccinated are not relevant in the epidemiology of COVID-19."

People who are vaccinated have a lower risk of severe disease but are still a relevant part of the pandemic. It is therefore wrong and dangerous to speak of a pandemic of the unvaccinated. Historically, both the USA and Germany have engendered negative experiences by stigmatising parts of the population for their skin colour or religion. I call on high-level officials and scientists to stop the inappropriate stigmatisation of unvaccinated people, who include our patients, colleagues, and other fellow citizens, and to put extra effort into bringing society together.[26]

The Best of Times, the Worst of Times

Even before the COVID-19 pandemic, we lived in deeply unequal times. Income and wealth disparities within and between countries had been rising for decades, largely as a result of government and central bank policies.

Since the global financial crisis of 2007–2008, most central banks have pursued policies aimed at inflating the value of financial assets. This has been great news for the top 10 percent of the population who own most of the assets but terrible news for the bottom 50 percent who barely own any. For example, when a central bank inflates the housing market, as most have been doing for decades, high-net-worth individuals see their personal wealth bloom as their property portfolios gain in value. People in the bottom 50 percent of the population not only don't benefit because they don't own a home, they have to pay more in rent, leaving them with even less disposable income and even less possibility of owning their own home.

Central bank policies have also concentrated wealth in another way: by making debt exceptionally cheap for the extremely wealthy. As interest rates have fallen close to zero, or in the case of Europe and Japan below zero, the rich have been able to access debt almost free of charge while middle and lower classes have continued having to pay much higher levels of interest on their credit card debt and consumer loans. This huge disparity in the cost of debt has allowed wealthy individuals to buy up assets and large companies to buy up their smaller rivals at virtually no cost.

Central banks' zero or (in the case of Europe and Japan) negative interest rate policies have also fueled inflation, as the former president of the Federal Reserve regional bank in Kansas, Thomas Hoenig, warned they would more than a decade ago. Hoenig ended up retiring from the Fed in late 2011. After that, a reputation crystalized around him as the man who got it wrong, as Christopher

Leonard writes in the *Politico* article, "The Fed's Doomsday Prophet Has a Dire Warning About Where We're Headed":

> *He is remembered as something like a cranky Old Testament prophet who warned incessantly, and incorrectly, about one thing: the threat of coming inflation.*
>
> *But this version of history isn't true. While Hoenig was concerned about inflation, that isn't what solely what drove him to lodge his string of dissents. The historical record shows that Hoenig was worried primarily that the Fed was taking a risky path that would deepen income inequality, stoke dangerous asset bubbles and enrich the biggest banks over everyone else. He also warned that it would suck the Fed into a money-printing quagmire that the central bank would not be able to escape without destabilizing the entire financial system.*
>
> *On all of these points, Hoenig was correct. And on all of these points, he was ignored. We are now living in a world that Hoenig warned about.* [27]

As returns on financial assets have exploded in recent decades, salaries have stagnated (except for CEOs and other white-collar executives, of course). A recent article in the journal *American Affairs* reported that $34 trillion of real equity wealth, in 2017 dollars, was created between 1989 and 2017. Just 25 percent of that new wealth creation was the result of economic growth. Nearly half of it (44 percent) was the result of a reallocation of corporate equity to shareholders at the expense of worker compensation. [28]

A similar trend has occurred across all Western economies. By 2019 the backlash had begun. Spontaneous protests erupted across the global north and the global south, from Paris to Beirut to Hong Kong to Santiago de Chile and to Bogota. Many governments were caught on the back foot. But then along came COVID-19 and the government-imposed lockdowns, which not only made it more difficult for workers to protest but have also supercharged the forces driving poverty and inequality around the world.

While hundreds of millions of workers lost their jobs and millions of small businesses went belly-up, large companies, financial institutions, and wealthy investors were bailed out by the central banks. Many of the small businesses that have survived have lost a large share of their customers and revenues.

Again, it was largely vulnerable populations that bore the brunt of the economic pain. A study in the UK found that Black, Asian, and minority ethnic (BAME) migrants were more likely to suffer job loss during the COVID-19 lockdown than UK-born White Brits. And even though White Brits were more likely to reduce their work hours during the pandemic than BAME migrants, they were less likely to experience income loss and increased financial hardship.[29]

As US journalist Alex Gutentag chronicled in her article "Revolt of the Essential Workers," the lockdowns themselves have already created a two-tier society:

> *When "two weeks to flatten the curve" began, the workforce was split in two: Some were defined as "essential" workers, and others as "nonessential." The "nonessential" ordered delivery from home while farmhands harvested crops, workers in meatpacking plants processed and packaged products, truckers shipped food across the country, cooks prepared dishes, Doordash "dashers" dropped off takeout on doorstops, and sanitation workers picked up the trash. This division allowed the professional class to be protected from exposure to the virus and set the stage for a two-tier society.[30]*

Wealthy individuals and companies were not just protected from exposure to the virus; they were also insulated from the economic pain of the pandemic-induced lockdowns. As the 2020 financial crisis deepened, the Federal Reserve printed trillions of dollars to bail out investors in highly leveraged hedge funds and real estate investment trusts that were imploding. It rescued asset holders whose stocks were plunging, as well as speculators in some of the riskiest asset classes, such as junk bonds. The wealthier they were, the more they received. A similar playbook was used by major central banks all over the world.

Between the start of the pandemic, in March 2020, and October 2021 the four largest central banks—the Federal Reserve, the European Central Bank, the People's Bank of China, and the Bank of Japan—increased their combined balance sheets by a staggering $10 trillion, from around $20 trillion to $30.8 trillion. The European Central Bank and the Federal Reserve accounted for over three-quarters of the new money printing.[31]

To borrow from Dickens, these are the best of times (for a privileged few) and the worst of times (for most of the rest of us). The economic fallout of successive lockdowns has already plunged anywhere from 143 million to 163 million people into poverty worldwide. At the same time, tech companies like Amazon, Alphabet, and Microsoft have posted record profits. Some of the world's biggest banks are earning more than ever before as equity markets explode, aided by an upsurge in mergers and acquisitions and unprecedented monetary and fiscal support programs.[32] As Gutentag notes, when lockdowns began, we were "all in this together," except that just about every government and central bank policy since then has widened inequality, crippled the middle class, and further enriched the rich.

To compound matters, prices of essential goods, including food and energy, are soaring worldwide due to unprecedented central bank money printing, postlockdown pent-up demand, supply chain shocks, and worker shortages. In October, consumer price inflation in the United States reached a 30-year high of 6.2 percent. In the European Union it hit 4.4 percent in October, its highest level since 2008. In my own country of residence, Spain, it reached 6.7 percent in November, the fastest annual pace of inflation since 1989. In the Netherlands it reached a near-40-year high. In some large emerging economies, such as Brazil and Turkey, inflation is already in the double digits. Many of the poorest on the planet, having already suffered the carnage of 2020, are now witnessing another savage cutback in their standard of living.

Meanwhile, the greatest upward wealth transfer in modern history continues apace. In the United States the top 1 percent of earners now holds more wealth than the entire middle class, according to data from the Federal Reserve.[33] The richest 10 percent now own 90 percent of stocks.

The widespread introduction of vaccine mandates and vaccine passports threaten to exacerbate this trend even further by creating a permanent underclass that is effectively banished from the formal economy. In the United States thousands of people are losing their jobs every day due to vaccine mandates for workers. When Italy's government introduced its "no jab, no job" ruling, an estimated 3.8 million workers were suspended without pay in one day. Yet the story barely made the international news.

These workers have suffered great personal cost, yet many of them (including in vital strategic sectors, such as logistics, law enforcement, and the military) are refusing to be cowed. Thousands of US workers are taking industrial action on a whole host of issues, including vaccine passports. The biggest class struggle of our lives has begun. As Russell Brand, British comedian and social commentator, put it, "we are no longer talking about rich versus poor; we are talking about a tiny percentage versus basically everyone."

Since the start of the pandemic, the Institute for Policy Studies has partnered with Americans for Tax Fairness to trace the rocketing growth of US billionaire wealth. By October 18, 2021, the combined wealth of the billionaire class had surged by 70 percent, or $2.1 trillion, during the pandemic. The billionaire class is now worth a staggering $5 trillion—roughly the same as the entire gross domestic product (GDP) of the world's third largest economy, Japan. It's not just the wealth of US billionaires that has grown; so have their numbers. In March of 2020, there were 614 Americans with 10-figure bank accounts. By October 2021, there were 745.

Even more alarming, the wealth of the top five billionaires—Elon Musk, Jeff Bezos, Bill Gates, Oracle cofounder Larry Ellison, and Google cofounder Larry Page—has grown even more quickly than the US billionaire class as a whole. Musk's wealth grew by a staggering 750 percent between March 2020 and October 2021, from $24.6 billion to $209 billion. Bezos' wealth grew by a more modest 70 percent, Gates' by 35 percent, Ellison's by 111 percent, and Page's by 137 percent. Together, these five men are worth more than $750 billion.

It's worth noting that all five of these billionaires minted their money in Silicon Valley, as did the next two on the list, Mark Zuckerberg (6th) and Sergey Brin (7th). Their net worth has skyrocketed, thanks largely to the breakneck digitization of the global economy facilitated by the COVID-19-induced lockdowns and other restrictions.[34] It has also benefited from the huge bailouts and stimulus programs unleashed by the Federal Reserve and other central banks, which have massively increased the market capitalization of their companies. Now, these tech billionaires stand to reap even more dividends from the business opportunities opened up by the vaccine passports. One of them (Bill Gates) has even been working behind the scenes to facilitate their rollout.

The vaccine passports and mandates will allow the billionaire class not only to continue expanding their wealth but also to entrench their power and control over the rest of us. But as the next chapter will show, even the best-laid plans can go awry.

CHAPTER FOUR

Untold Consequences

WHEN PUBLIC AUTHORITIES all over the world make it impossible for a critical mass of the population to participate in society or the economy, there are going to be consequences, many of them unintended. One obvious consequence is an acute labor shortfall. When that happens in economies already struggling with labor shortages, the effects are magnified (a situation we'll return to momentarily).

In the case of the COVID-19 pandemic, labor shortages also exacerbated a global supply-chain crisis that has made it difficult for businesses to procure the basic components they need to manufacture products that consumers and businesses are increasingly desperate to buy. In the UK, for example, small businesses are even struggling to get hold of items as basic and essential as cardboard.[1]

Of course, there are many reasons for this once-in-a-generation supply-chain crisis; the pandemic response is only the most obvious and impactful. When the virus was declared a pandemic in February 2020, countries responded by closing their borders and implementing lockdowns. Factories, construction sites, restaurants, and shops were forced to shut their doors. Governments temporarily closed or significantly reduced capacity at ports around the world. Demand for consumer goods—and all the raw materials and labor that go into them—fell off a cliff.

Against this backdrop, container carriers had no means of gauging future demand and did the only rational thing: They slashed capacity. The immediate consequence was widespread vessel cancellations. Within a matter of weeks, global supply chains had snapped.

As we have since learned, it is a lot easier to press the pause button on the global economy than it is to release it. Formerly shuttered factories took time to get moving once again. Raw materials were in short supply. As a result, when economies began reopening in the second half of 2020, there was a massive shortfall of the basic components global consumer goods manufacturers needed to assemble their products. For example, a dearth of silicon chips (processors and other semiconductor components) prevented automakers from finishing many of their models and the supply of new vehicles to the market plunged.

The problem was not just one of supply but also distribution. The reopening of economies led to a massive surge in pent-up demand for raw materials, components, and finished consumer products, but there weren't enough trucks, freight trains, planes, or ships in the world to transport all the timber, semiconductors, car parts, bikes, trainers, petrol, whisky, and other things businesses and consumers were clamoring for.

The Deep Roots of the Supply-Chain Crisis

There are deeper-rooted reasons for the supply-chain crisis, including the trend among multinational corporations to offshore and outsource their production processes to countries with lower costs of labor, such as China, Vietnam, and Mexico. This allowed them to book huge profits, but it also made them more vulnerable to a supply-chain shock. Many of these same companies also bet big on just-in-time (JIT) manufacturing by holding low inventories and having necessary component parts delivered right as they're needed for a particular step in assembly. This meant that when the shock came, they did not have spare capacity to ride it out.

The ongoing trade war between the world's two superpowers, the United States and China, has also made matters a lot worse, as *Business Insider* reports.

In September 2020, the Trump White House imposed export restrictions on SMIC, China's biggest chipmaker, forcing it to source parts elsewhere and reconfiguring supply chains in the process. Meanwhile, companies buying their chips from SMIC had to go elsewhere, only to find that alternative chipmakers were already at full capacity.

America struggled to rely on its own production, as lead US semiconductor giant Intel struggled with its own production problems. And some firms have been hoarding chips, claims TSMC's CEO Mark Lui, making the chip crunch even worse.

The Biden administration has been enlisting its allies to freeze China out from the technological equipment it needs, making sourcing even harder for the country.

This all happened after the pandemic shut down semiconductor manufacturing operations for months in 2020, leading to spikes in the prices of new and used cars and shortages of all kinds of electronics.[2]

And of course, there is another huge factor exacerbating the supply-chain crisis, as I mentioned above: an acute—and in many places worsening—labor shortage. Vaccine mandates and passports are making those shortages far more severe.

For example, the ports of Los Angeles and Long Beach, which handle around 40 percent of all US container imports, are suffering from both a shortage of truck drivers and terminal mechanics. As a result, there aren't enough trucks to remove containers from the rail yards. This has created an unprecedented backlog of empty containers that, in turn, prevent cranes from removing containers from the waiting ships. That backlog is unlikely to ease until the summer of 2022, said Gene Seroka, executive director of the Port of Los Angeles, in mid-December. At that time the port was still short of around 4,000 truckers, which was continuing to exacerbate the port's surfeit of empty containers.[3]

"From Los Angeles to Felixstowe, England; to Dubai, United Arab Emirates; to Shenzhen, China, the world is witnessing delays and shortages of everything from toys to turkeys," Guy Platten, the secretary general of the International Chamber of Shipping, pointed out in a November 2021 *New York Times* op-ed. "At the root of this crisis is a transport sector that is buckling under the strain of COVID-era conditions. Workers who drive the trucks, fly the

planes, and crew the ships responsible for moving all these goods—
around $19 trillion of world trade annually—have been stretched to
the breaking point. Governments have been too slow to act."[4]

A month earlier, a Twitter post by Ryan Petersen, the founder and
CEO of the logistics firm Flexport, perfectly illustrated this point. On
October 21, Petersen rented a boat and took the leader of one of Flexport's biggest partners on a 3-hour tour of Los Angeles' Long Beach
port, ground zero of the United States' months-long supply-chain
crisis. What Peterson learned was that on that day alone "there were
76 ships waiting at the Port, with 430,000 container cargoes worth
$26 billion," yet only seven out of hundreds of the port's cranes were
actually operating and fewer than a dozen containers were unloaded.[5]

By late November, Bloomberg was reporting that the huge back-
logs at US ports had begun to clear, but that wasn't strictly true. The
waiting container ships were still out there—but many of them were
out of sight, and also seemingly out of mind. As the trade publication
Hellenic Shipping News reported, many of the ships were over the
horizon, where they couldn't be seen (and as such weren't counted),
thanks to the successful implementation of a new queuing system:

> *If you include all of the container ships physically at anchor on
> Tuesday off LA/LB, plus the ships in holding patterns within
> 40 miles of the ports, which were counted in the previous queuing
> system, plus all the ships waiting further afield that are now
> technically in the queue under the new system, then 93 container
> vessels were waiting for berths at Los Angeles/Long Beach on
> Tuesday, a new all-time high.* [6]

It's a perfect example of how government, with a little help from
media, has tried to conceal the stark reality of the crisis. As *Hellenic
Shipping News* suggested, "perhaps politicians were more interested
in erasing a politically nettlesome photo op—attention-grabbing
imagery of idle container ships stretching off into the distance"—
than actually tackling its hugely complex underlying causes.
Unfortunately, when governments do act, they often make the crisis
worse rather than better.

Making the Great Resignation Even Greater

Even before the Biden government unveiled its vaccine mandate in September 2021, a record number of Americans were quitting their jobs. The Job Openings and Labor Turnover Survey found that 2.9 percent of Americans quit their jobs in August, the highest figure since the survey began in 2000. This trend was dubbed the Great Resignation, or the Big Quit, and is happening for many reasons, including shoddy work conditions, intensifying workplace surveillance, and Victorian-era differentials between the salaries and bonuses rewarded at the top and the peanuts handed out at the bottom. Due to the high demand for workers across the economy, some low-paid workers are looking for better paid jobs in other sectors. Others are opting to retire early.

And then, of course, there are the vaccine mandates. As they have come into effect, the Big Quit has got even bigger. In September, the number of people quitting grew even more, reaching a new record high of 4.4 million—equivalent to 3 percent of all Americans. The hardest hit sectors were leisure and hospitality, trade, transportation and utilities, and professional services and retail. The fact that many workers in the trade, transportation, and utilities sector are leaving their posts should be a major cause for concern, given the ongoing supply chain and energy crises.

Many Western economies are also suffering from a dearth of truck drivers. France is short of around 40–50,000, Germany 80,000, and Spain 15,000.[7] The UK urgently needs 100,000 more truckers if it is to meet demand, according to the trade group Road Haulage Association (RHA).[8] If it doesn't, the country risks suffering even more severe energy and food shortages. However, the UK's truck driver shortage is a result of a number of factors including, of course, Brexit, which led many foreign truck drivers to head back home; the huge backlog in truck driver tests due to the pandemic, meaning tens of thousands of potential new drivers have been unable to join the industry; and the fact that even before the pandemic more people were leaving the industry than coming into it. Many young people simply don't want to work in such a hard, lonely, and often poorly paid job.

In the United States, truckers can earn even less than the statutory minimum ($2.13) earned by waiters with no hope of tips making up the difference, explains Ryan Johnson, a 20-year truck driver, in his article "How Truckers Are Paid":

> Truck drivers, farm workers, and restaurant staff are exempt from the Fair Labor Standards Act (FLSA). While many states have corrected some of the worst abuses against farm workers and restaurant staff (and many have not), the one profession that is still untouched by any reform is trucking, largely because of federal interstate commerce exemptions. Trucking companies will use every loophole they can to not pay their workers, and the laws are so loose that employers can literally make up the rules as they go . . .
>
> Truck drivers can legally be paid in multiple ways. This is true for all levels of trucking, either direct employee, "independent contractor" owner ops leased to a company, or owner operators under their own authority. They can be paid hourly, a percentage of the load, by the mile, flat rate, or a combination of all of these. But in all of these cases, the wage laws that apply to 99% of the public who are paid hourly do not apply to trucker pay.[9]

Mandating vaccines for the millions of truck drivers across the United States will make matters a lot worse. The country is already short of around 80,000 truckers compared to before the pandemic. But that number could explode if the federal government pushes through its vaccine mandate without exempting the haulage industry. If Biden's January 4 vaccine deadline is enforced, the industry will lose 37 percent of its truckers, or 2.5 million people, according to a survey by the American Trucking Association (ATA), the country's largest trucking trade group.

"We've tried to be very clear to the administration—I understand the logic behind it—but if you do this, these are the consequences," said ATA President Chris Spear in testimony to the US Congress. "So, if you're trying to solve the supply chain problem, you're actually compounding it and actually hurting the very problem you're trying to fix . . . 37 percent of the drivers not only said 'no,' but 'hell no.'"

A worsening supply-chain crisis not only means that products will take longer to reach businesses and end-consumers but also that when they do, they will be more expensive. This will heap even further pressure on the tight margins of many of the world's already struggling, heavily indebted small and medium-sized businesses.

The trucking industry reflects a broader trend in the United States, which is that blue-collar, customer-facing industries are seeing the biggest exoduses. By November 2021 manufacturing quit rates were up 78 percent compared to February 2020, according to Nick Bunker, economic research director for North America at the Indeed Hiring Lab. By contrast, the number of people quitting in a traditionally white-collar, office-based industry, such as the financial activities sector, was up only 5 percent. In other words, many of the low-paid essential workers who were lionized for keeping the economy alive last year are leaving their jobs in droves while well-paid white-collar workers are largely staying put.[10]

While many of those who left their jobs in the summer did so over reasons of pay, benefits, and working conditions, by the autumn the main motivation had shifted to the vaccine mandates, according to Ronald J. Pugliese Jr., a union, labor, and employment lawyer:

> *The government mandates on health care workers, educational employees, and federal government employees have not persuaded people to take the vaccine as expected. In fact, it looks like more people are choosing to leave their jobs or ask for accommodations rather than submit to forced vaccination . . .*
>
> *Now we are stuck with a divided society, a labor crisis, a supply chain crisis, soaring inflation, low worker morale, a low vaccination rate, a pandemic that will not quit, and millions of Americans out of work. Oh, and to top it off, up to a third of Chicago police officers could be placed on unpaid leave over the city's vaccine mandate. This is happening in a city where crime is out of control. Do the residents of Chicago, and other major cities, really want their police forces cut in half over their vaccination status? I know I don't.[11]*

This is one of the most important side effects of the vaccine mandates and passports: At a time when the economy needs more qualified workers than ever, millions are being threatened with the sack for refusing to take a vaccine that offers little hope of controlling, let alone vanquishing, the virus. This is going to make life even harder for the legions of struggling small and medium-size businesses. To make matters even worse, as economic conditions decline, many of the public workers we depend on to keep society functioning—police officers, soldiers, refuse collectors, firefighters, teachers, coastguard officers, customs officials—are also being sidelined.

The Final Straw for Health Care Systems

Vaccine passports and mandates not only risk exacerbating the global supply-chain crisis, in the process pushing inflation even higher, they also threaten to break many countries' national health care systems. Many of these systems were already struggling prior to the pandemic, were brought to the brink during the course of the pandemic, and could well reach the breaking point, as a consequence of mandates and passports. Once again, one of the biggest issues is acute staff shortages. Millions of frontline health care workers around the world, including doctors and nurses, midwives, radiographers and ambulance drivers, have been forced to choose between taking the vaccine and losing their job. Many have chosen the latter.

A significant number of those health care workers already have some degree of immunity as a result of previous COVID-19 infection. Numerous studies suggest natural infection provides broader, longer-lasting immunity than vaccines.[12] But in many jurisdictions, including the United States and the United Kingdom, naturally acquired immunity doesn't count. You are either vaccinated or you are not; there is no other way. The EU, to its credit, still recognizes natural immunity, but it only buys you six months of eligibility for the Green Pass. After that you need the vaccine. And by the beginning of 2022, some EU Member States, such as France and Belgium, were thinking of abandoning all recognition of naturally acquired immunity as well as negative PCR test results. Health care workers were already leaving their jobs in droves before the vaccine mandates, for a host of reasons, including the glaring (and growing) disparity between executive pay and the salaries of frontline workers. In the United States, hospital execs have received record pay and bonuses during the pandemic while the nurses who have been holding the fort, at risk to their own health, got virtually nothing. It's a similar story in England and Wales, where nurses were offered a paltry pay rise of just 3 percent; that's less than the rate of consumer price inflation, meaning they will actually be getting a pay cut in real terms. The Royal College of Nursing, the country's largest nurses' trade union, called the pay deal a "bitter blow."

"Hospitals and other parts of the NHS are struggling to recruit nurses and health care support workers," said Royal College of Nursing (RCN) General Secretary and Chief Executive Pat Cullen. "The government has been warned that many more are on the verge of leaving. With today's decision, ministers have made it even harder to provide safe care to patients."[13]

Staff shortages in the NHS were already acute before COVID-19, after many nurses and doctors from mainland Europe packed their bags and headed back to their countries following Brexit. Many of the remaining nurses and doctors are facing burnout.

It's a vicious cycle that is crippling health care systems around the world, from the UK to the United States, to France and Australia. The worse the staff shortages get, the more nurses and doctors end up succumbing to mental and physical exhaustion, further exacerbating the shortages.

The vaccine mandates appear to be the final straw. A sudden wave of dismissals and resignations of unvaccinated staff is making it even harder for overstretched hospitals to treat patients of COVID-19 and other serious conditions, especially as winter brings higher caseloads. Waiting lists for non-COVID-19 interventions are growing at an alarming rate at the same time that caseloads for COVID-19 as well as other acute illnesses are surging.

In the UK, almost six million people were waiting for hospital treatment at the end of September 2021, the highest number since the National Health System (NHS) began collecting these records in August 2007.[14] Over three hundred thousand patients were having to wait more than a year for hospital treatment, more than double the number a year earlier. The number of people waiting more than 12 hours in the emergency room surged by 40 percent between

September and October 2021 alone. Twenty times more people were waiting over six weeks for vital scans that can diagnose heart disease compared to the number prior to the pandemic, according to the British Heart Foundation in November 2021.[15]

These system failings are already costing lives. Research by the *Financial Times* (*FT*) found that 2,047 more people died in the second week of November 2021 than during the same period between 2015 and 2019. Just over half of these people (1,197) had COVID-19 on their death certificates. This "raises the possibility that since the summer more people have been losing their lives as a result of the strains on the NHS or lack of early diagnosis of serious illness." The most frequent causes of extra deaths were cardiovascular disease and strokes, raising the stark possibility that vaccine injuries may have played a part (though this connection was avoided in the *FT* article).[16]

Of course, the UK's health care system has been in crisis for years, after decades of mismanagement, underfunding, and stealth privatization. Unfortunately, just about everything the UK government is doing right now is further deepening the crisis, which in turn is creating yet more opportunities to further privatize the system.

On November 11, the Department of Health and Social Care pushed through a vaccine mandate for care workers in England, propelling as many as 70,000 workers out of the sector, according to Nadra Ahmed, the executive chair of the National Care Association (NCA).[17] Care leaders begged the health secretary, Sajid Javid, a former investment banker, for an 11th hour reprieve, but to no avail.

Care homes were already facing their most acute staffing shortage on record prior to the mandate, with some 170,000 vacancies.[18] The vaccine mandate has further exacerbated those shortages, forcing many care homes to cut back on their services. Methodist Homes (MHA), the UK's largest charity care provider with 90 care homes and 6,000 employees, announced in November that it was closing around 7.5 percent of its care homes to new admissions. The care provider estimates that around 750 care homes may have already stopped taking new admissions due to the staffing shortages.[19]

"This means fewer older people are able to get the care they need to live the good life they deserve, and more older people find themselves unable to leave hospital after a spell as an inpatient," said Sam Monaghan, chief executive of MHA. The vaccine mandate has also heaped further pressure on the overstretched NHS, as more and more care homes refuse to take patients from hospitals.[20]

NHS staff in England will face their own "no jab, no job" mandate in early 2022, which could lead to the additional loss of up to 80,000 workers, including many doctors, nurses, and other frontline staff. Naturally, if that were to come to pass, it would be even harder for the NHS to deliver the basic health services English patients need.

The British government doesn't seem overly concerned about that prospect, presumably because the worse the system performs, the more opportunities will open up for private health companies, many of them US-based, to fill the gaps. And many of those health companies have close ties to the governing Conservative Party. In a survey by the online news platform *Open Democracy*, 40 percent of the patients who responded said they "were told that the NHS simply can't offer them the treatment they need. Half of these patients—20 percent of all patients—said an NHS worker then told them they would instead have to pay privately for the treatment they needed."[21]

In the Canadian province of British Colombia, the government's vaccine mandate for health care workers, implemented in November 2021, put so much pressure on hospital staffing that by late December the same government announced it was considering "allowing" some infected doctors and nurses to return to work. Authorities in the province of Quebec had already taken this step while the province of Alberta had allowed unvaccinated workers back on the job, as long as they agreed to undergo regular testing.[22]

It's a similar story in the United States where many hospitals, be they privately funded or publicly subsidized through the Medicare or Medicaid systems, have been stretched to the breaking point, particularly in the rural heartlands. In October 2021, the Biden administration imposed vaccine mandates for workers in most health care institutions that receive Medicare or Medicaid reimbursement, including hospitals, ambulatory surgical settings, dialysis facilities, and home health agencies. By the middle of the month, around 41 percent of all hospitals in the country had imposed a vaccine mandate on their staff.

Some executives at rural hospitals worry the vaccine mandate will exacerbate a labor shortage that could be described as severe, even prior to the pandemic. "Some hospitals have already cut back, delayed, or eliminated services, such as elective surgeries, labor, and delivery, and other inpatient care," according to the independent nonprofit Pew Charitable Trusts. There are fears that some hospitals will even have to close their doors.

"I've talked with administrators of hospitals that have estimated anywhere from 3 percent to as much as 20 percent of their workforce may have to quit their jobs if they're required to have the vaccine as a condition of their employment," said Brock Slabach, chief operations officer for the National Rural Health Association, a nonprofit representing rural hospitals and clinics as well as doctors, nurses, and administrators. "In a rural hospital, that could be two, maybe three nurses, which could cripple their ability to meet the demands of patient care."[23]

These problems are not unique to rural America. In late November 2021, Mount Sinai South Nassau in New York announced the temporary closure of the freestanding Long Beach Emergency Department due to nursing staff shortages caused by the state COVID-19 vaccination mandate.[24] Staff shortages also led to temporary hospital closures in the upstate New York cities of Syracuse and Buffalo.[25]

Health care systems on mainland Europe are also buckling. In France, where more than 3,000 unvaccinated health care workers were suspended in September 2021, one in five beds was out of action at the end of October due to acute staff shortages. As a fresh wave of COVID-19 infections gathered steam, *France 24* reported that many nurses and nursing assistants no longer had the strength to continue. Resignations and absenteeism were threatening to derail a hospital system that was already stretched to breaking point. Thierry Amouroux, a spokesperson for the National Union of Nursing Professionals (SNPI), said he had never seen anything like it in his 40-year career.

We have always closed beds from July to allow staff to go on leave. But this is the first time that we have not been able to reopen the beds at the start of the school year.[26]

It is testament to the folly and hubris of our leadership class that many of the heroic doctors, nurses, care-assistants, and other front-line health care staff who were lionized during the early waves of the COVID-19 pandemic are now being forced out of work for refusing to take vaccines that provide little in the way of protection from infection or transmission.

IT System Vulnerabilities

Another important source of systemic fragility is IT. Large swathes of the globe have undergone 10 or 15 years' worth of digital transformation in the space of just two. This has brought some key benefits, such as greater speed and convenience of digital transactions. Virtual communication platforms such as Zoom have made it possible for millions of office workers to work from home during the pandemic. But it has also made the IT systems and networks we depend upon for almost everything more fragile and vulnerable to crime.

As almost everything was pushed online, including work, communication, payment methods, government processes, and, even to a certain extent, health care, many criminals did the only logical thing: They migrated online, too. Ransomware—malicious software that threatens to publish private data or renders it inaccessible unless a bounty is paid—has become increasingly popular among criminals since the pandemic began. Targets can range from small businesses and nonprofit organizations to utility providers, food suppliers, government agencies, and global banks.

In March 2021, Spain's employment service (SEPE) was hit by a ransomware attack that paralyzed all of its online processes, resulting in the suspension of virtually all activities at the organization's 700 offices. The attack disrupted the payments of unemployment benefits to some of the 2.73 million people who depended on SEPE. After roughly a week, the system was restored after the government paid the hackers an unspecified amount of money to end the siege.[27]

Two months later, Colonial Pipeline, the United States' largest petroleum pipeline, fell prey to a ransomware attack that brought down the computerized equipment managing the pipeline. The attack disrupted a major supply of fuel to the East Coast for roughly a week before the $4.4 million ransom was paid (much of which was later recovered) and the system restored. According to inside sources, the system was breached by a single leaked password.[28]

This is one of the main reasons for the rising fragility of the IT systems on which we are increasingly reliant: The easiest way to pull off a hack is to have a mole on the inside. And that is nigh-on impossible to prevent, given how many disgruntled employees many large companies have on their payroll, or formerly on their payroll. The rising threat is also being driven by the increasing technological sophistication and capability of hackers. The work-from-home revolution has also increased vulnerabilities. Often neither the companies nor their employees consider the security implications of working from home until it's too late.

Banks are an increasingly popular target, particularly in emerging economies where financial institutions have fewer funds to dedicate to IT security. At the end of October 2021, Pakistan's third largest lender, the National Bank of Pakistan (NBP), suffered a huge cyber-attack that put its online banking system out of action for more than 48 hours. NBP is one of three banks in Pakistan deemed to be systemically important at a domestic level. As a column in the *Express Tribune*, Pakistan's only internationally affiliated newspaper, noted, this means it is officially "too big to fail. The entire national economy could collapse if something goes wrong at NBP."[29]

Even short-lived bank outages can cause serious problems for consumers and business customers, including lack of access to one's own money and financial services. They are happening more and more frequently in countries across the globe, whether due to internal IT issues, external outages, or cybercrime.

For example, the online banking system of Mexico's largest lender, BBVA, went down three times in 2021. On each occasion the bank's 24 million customers were unable to use the bank's ATMs, its mobile app, or in-store payments. Two of the outages took place on a Sunday, meaning customers could not even avail themselves of the lender's in-branch cash services. The bank blamed the first Sunday outage on an internal system update failure and was at pains to assure customers that their financial data was not compromised. A month later, the system went down again.

Other banks that have suffered serious outages include Ecuador's largest lender, Banco Pichincha, whose IT system was brought down by a ransomware attack for several days in October. Venezuela's largest lender, Banco de Venezuela, was also taken out by a cyberattack in September, which the Venezuelan government blamed on the United States government. The bank's 16 million customers had no access to any digital banking services for five days.

It is not just banks in emerging markets that are suffering cyberattacks; so, too, are many big banks in advanced economies. One of New Zealand's largest lenders, Kiwibank, and ANZ Bank, Australia's third largest lender, both suffered distributed denial-of-service (DDoS) attacks in 2021, leading to a spate of IT system outages.

During the same year, Mizuho Bank, one of Japan's three mega banks, experienced so many IT system failures—the equivalent of almost one every month—that it ended up costing the jobs of Mizuho Financial Group CEO Tatsufumi Sakai and Mizuho Bank President Koji Fujiwara.[30] Another giant Asian lender, Singapore-based DBS Bank, suffered its worst outage in 10 years at the end of November. This is a bank that prides itself on its technological prowess, having picked up the Euromoney's hotly contested "World's Best Digital Bank" accolade on more than one occasion. The bank's ambition is to become "digital to the core." Yet for over 48 hours many of its customers were unable to access online banking services.[31]

In the UK, nary a week goes by without the mobile app and/or online platform of at least one high street bank going down. On just one day in November, three large banks—Lloyds, Halifax, and Bank of Scotland, all belonging to the Lloyds Banking Group—encountered problems with their mobile apps and internet banking services, leaving many customers unable to access their online accounts.[32] Two weeks earlier, another big bank, Barclays, suffered a nationwide outage that left thousands of customers fuming.[33] A week earlier, it was the turn of HSBC and NatWest.

On the other side of the Atlantic, Bank of America suffered a major outage in October 2021 that left thousands of its customers locked out of their online accounts for hours on end. Like most banks, the company says it has seen a huge increase in digital banking, with 85 percent of customers using digital channels for deposits.

These bank outages may have happened for a whole gamut of reasons, from internal glitches to sophisticated hacks, to server outages, but one thing they all highlight is the inherent fragility of banks' IT systems, at a time when cash is being hurriedly replaced by digital banking services (see chapter 6).

It is not just banks that are falling prey to cyberattacks. So, too, are many major government agencies, insurance firms, credit reporting companies, cryptocurrency exchanges, central banks, and even the most sophisticated tech companies on the planet, such as Microsoft, Google, and Facebook. And if they can't protect their own systems from attack, who can?

A Digital Pandemic?

The vulnerability of key IT systems and networks has not escaped the attention of the World Economic Forum, which is spearheading the accelerated shift toward a digital economy. In July 2020, the organization held a cyberattack simulation titled Cyber Polygon 2020, whose central theme, ominously, was "Digital Pandemic." During the event 120 of the largest Russian and international organizations from 29 countries joined the technical training to respond to a simulated attack, aimed at hacking company data and undermining its reputation. The participants included many of the world's biggest banks. One of the keynote speakers was former UK Prime Minister Tony Blair, who told the event's participants that Digital Identity would form an inevitable part of the digital ecosystem being constructed around us, and so governments should work with technology companies to regulate their use.

For the 2021 edition of the event, an estimated 5 million people from 57 nations tuned into the live stream, which featured, as the website states, "global leaders and experts, including Mikhail Mishustin, Prime Minister of the Russian Federation, and Klaus Schwab, Founder and Executive Chairman, World Economic Forum

as well as top officials from INTERPOL, ICANN, Visa, IBM, Sber-
bank, MTS and other organizations." Also participating were "state
and law enforcement agencies, financial, educational and health
care institutions, organizations from the IT, telecom, energy, metal,
chemical, aerospace engineering and other industries."

The participants were split into two teams: The Red Team simulated a supply-chain cyberattack while the Blue Team had to contain
it as best it could. On the event's website is a stark warning that in
light of the digitalization trends largely spurred by the COVID-19
crisis, "a single vulnerable link is enough to bring down the entire
system, just like the domino effect."[34] A promotional video for
the event posted on the World Economic Forum's (WEF) official
YouTube channel warned that "a cyberattack with COVID-19-like
characteristics would spread faster and further than any biological
virus. Its reproductive rate would be around 10 times greater than
what we've experienced with the coronavirus."[35]

The question some people are asking is whether Cyber Polygon
2021 will prove to be as prophetic as Event 201, the coronavirus pandemic simulation exercise the World Economic Forum organized
in partnership with the Johns Hopkins Center for Health Security
and the Bill and Melinda Gates Foundation just months before the
outbreak of COVID-19.[36]

Interestingly, just as Cyber Polygon 2021 was about to start, a real
cyberattack occurred. The Russian-based cybercriminal organization REvil launched a massive ransomware attack that encrypted 60
managed service providers by exploiting a zero-day vulnerability in
the Kaseya VSA remote management platform. In what technology
news website *Bleeping Computer* described as the "largest ransomware attack ever conducted," REvil was able to infect the computer
systems of more than 1,500 global organizations.[37]

It doesn't take a cyberattack for a vital IT system to go down and
cause chaos. Natural disasters or internal glitches can do just as much
damage. In June 2018, a hardware failure in Visa's card payment network in Western Europe left many consumers in the region unable to
pay for purchases for hours on end. When a category-five hurricane
ripped through Puerto Rico in 2017, the island's electronic payments

system went down for weeks, essentially turning the island into a cash-only economy. If you didn't have cash, you couldn't buy anything.[38]

There are more recent examples. On November 11, travelers at British airports were forced to wait hours at border control due to a national outage of the facilities' self-service e-gates. It was the third reported failure in three months. Using biometric identifiers, the e-passport gates can process as many as five passengers every 45 seconds, providing a fast and effective way to clear the border. When they fail, the work falls to staff on passport control desks. But the UK border force, like so many organizations these days, was suffering from an acute staff shortage.[39]

The unintended consequences of our pandemic response, including the vaccine mandates and vaccine passports, are making the delivery of basic goods and essential services more and more difficult, while many of the IT systems we depend upon are becoming more and more fragile. But it is not just the unintended consequences of vaccine mandates and passports we should worry about; it is also the intended consequences. They include an accelerating shift toward authoritarianism around the world.

"The world is becoming more authoritarian as nondemocratic regimes become even more brazen in their repression and many democratic governments suffer from backsliding by adopting their tactics of restricting free speech and weakening the rule of law, exacerbated by what threatens to become a 'new normal' of COVID-19 restrictions," warned the International Institute for Democracy and Electoral Assistance, a Sweden-based global nonprofit. The number of countries that are becoming "more authoritarian" by the group's calculus is three times the number of countries that are moving toward democracy. The year 2021 was the fifth consecutive year in which the trend has moved in that direction, the longest uninterrupted stretch of proauthoritarian developments since the IIDEA started tracking these metrics in 1975.[40]

If vaccine passports and digital IDs get a foothold, they threaten to significantly intensify this trend by ushering in an all-pervasive, tech-enabled, heavily centralized system of totalitarian social control and surveillance that threatens to obliterate what remains of our constitutional rights. Do you think I'm exaggerating? Read on.

CHAPTER FIVE

Rules for Thee, Not for Me

ON SATURDAY, OCTOBER 29, 2021, the heads of state of the world's 20 largest economies and their staff gathered for the G-20 meeting in Rome, just two weeks after Italy's government had passed one of the world's most draconian de facto vaccine mandates. To guarantee the "peaceful conduct" of the meeting (in the words of Italian press agency ANSA), a 10 square kilometer maximum security area was erected around Rome's Nuvolo, equipped with manned access gates, snipers at select points, and an antidrone system.[1] It was a perfect illustration of the gaping distance between the governors and the governed.

Two days later, many of the same heads of state converged on the city of Glasgow for the COP26 summit on climate change, where they were joined by thousands of environmental activists, NGO workers, and some of the world's richest billionaires, many of whom arrived on private jets. So, too, did many heads of state. Scotland's *Mail on Sunday* reported that as many as 400 landed at Glasgow's international airport, where they disgorged more than 1,000 VIPs and their staff, all for an event ostensibly aimed at "bring[ing] together world leaders to commit to urgent global climate action."[2]

The genuine environmentalists in attendance were not impressed. Private aircraft emit between 10 and 60 times as much carbon dioxide per passenger as scheduled flights, and up to 140 times as much as a diesel-powered train.

"It can't be stressed enough how bad private jets are for the environment—it is the worst way to travel by miles," said the European advocacy group Transport and Environment. "Private jets are very prestigious, but it is difficult to avoid the hypocrisy of using one while claiming to be fighting climate change."

But there was an even more egregious example of double standards on display, although it received much less attention in the legacy media: The 30,000 attendees, who had come from all corners of the world including countries with severe COVID-19 outbreaks, were not required to use the Scottish Government's vaccine passport system to enter the country or the conference. Instead, they were asked to take a daily lateral flow device test—a luxury not afforded to the six million people of Scotland, who must show a vaccine passport if they want to attend a nightclub or an indoor event with more than 500 people in the audience.

The Scottish Hospitality Group was enraged by the exemption for COP26. Stephen Montgomery, a spokesman for the group, said:

> *To have thousands of people descend on Glasgow from all around the world with no need for vaccine certification, it undermines the reason why we are doing this in the first place.*
>
> *Are the Government in the same situation as we are in that they cannot find the staff to police it or are they finally realising there is no point?*
>
> *Where is the bigger risk? 30,000 people from all over the world at the SEC or 400 people in a nightclub?*[3]

This is not the first time authorities in the UK have been accused of applying COVID-19 rules unevenly. In June, Boris Johnson's government granted quarantine exemptions to business leaders arriving from countries with high levels of infection. While everyone else had to spend 10 days in a quarantine hotel, well-connected business leaders were free to go about their business, as long as they submitted to a PCR test before and on their arrival in the country. To qualify, executives working at multinational companies simply have to apply for written permission from the government in advance of their journey, demonstrating that their work in the UK would "probably" preserve an existing UK-based business with at least 500 employees, or create a new one within two years.

"Yet again it is one rule for those at the top and another for everyone else," said the Labour Party's deputy leader, Angela Rayer. "This makes a total mockery of the sacrifices of the British people during this pandemic and this double standard is an insult to frontline workers that the British people will rightly be disgusted by."[4]

It seems clear that many governmental rules and policies set up to control the virus will serve only to widen the chasm between privileged citizens and the rest of society.

Do As I Say, Not As I Do

Politicians themselves have been flouting many of the emergency laws they have enacted over the past two years. The UK's former Health Minister Matt Hancock was forced to resign in June 2021 after being caught in flagrante with a married colleague at a time when the rest of the country was banned from hugging people from different households.[5] Professor Neil Ferguson, the renowned epidemiologist whose advice to the UK government had led to the first lockdown, continued meeting his mistress during the lockdown. In neither case were criminal charges filed.

In late November 2021, an even bigger scandal erupted when it emerged that in December 2020—when the UK's deadly third wave of coronavirus infections had led many local authorities to ban people from meeting indoors with members of other households—the prime minister's staffers had organized a Christmas party at 10 Downing Street. "Officials knocked back glasses of wine during a Christmas quiz and a Secret Santa while the rest of the country was forced to stay home," the *Daily Mirror* claimed in a report in late November. Since then, more reports have emerged of British government ministers and civil servants partying boozily while the rest of the country was banned from even meeting with members from other households.

There have been countless similar examples of "do as I say, not as I do" behavior among the political class across the world. The mayor of Washington, DC, Muriel Bowser, went maskless at a wedding reception less than a day after imposing a new mask mandate on the city's citizens. New Zealand's health minister, David Clark, also broke strict lockdown rules his government put in place.

The fact that many policymakers seem to believe they are above the laws they themselves are passing should be a major cause of public concern, especially given that governments around the world have awarded themselves unprecedented new emergency powers under the guise of combating the pandemic, as data collated from the COVID-19 Digital Rights Tracker and Civic Freedom Tracker shows. Many governments have used digital technologies to expand their control of the population. To monitor rule-breakers, 22 countries have used surveillance drones. Facial recognition programs have been expanded, internet censorship has intensified, and 13 countries have resorted to internet shutdowns.[6]

"The defining feature . . . of this great transformation that they are attempting to impose is that the mechanism which renders it formally possible is not a new body of laws, but a state of exception—in other words, not an affirmation of, but the suspension of constitutional guarantees," wrote the Italian philosopher Giorgio Agamben in the introduction to his collection of writings on the COVID-19 pandemic, *Where Are We Now: The Epidemic as Politics*.[7]

For most countries emergency powers are nothing new. They serve an important function, allowing governments to respond robustly and swiftly to temporary crises. But they are prone to overuse and abuse. And they are being used liberally by so-called liberal democracies and dictatorships alike. One problem is that most governments do not like to relinquish the temporary powers once they have served their purpose. In the United States, 39 temporary national emergencies were still in effect as of February 2020, one of which—Executive Order 12170, blocking Iranian government property after Iran's Islamic Revolution—dates all the way back to 1979.[8]

Arguably of even greater concern is the increasing use of so-called "emergency responses," warns Luke Kemp, a research associate at the Centre for the Study of Existential Risk at the University of Cambridge, in a BBC article titled "The 'Stomp Reflex': When Governments Abuse Emergency Powers":

> *[This is] exceptional legislation that is not designated as an emergency power, but is either passed during or in reaction to a threat. Many of the counter-terrorism acts passed in the UK during the last two decades were ordinary legislation, but would make most emergency powers seem tame. Similarly, the current UK Police,*

Crime, Sentencing and Courts Bill contains what some critics consider to be sweeping provisions, but is being passed during a time that is less than ideal for public deliberation and scrutiny.

Many members of the public are too distracted or paralyzed by fear to question the motives behind the increasingly draconian rules or consider their potential long-term implications. As Agamben wrote in the early days of the pandemic, "For fear of getting sick, Italians are ready to sacrifice practically everything—their normal living conditions, their social relations, their jobs, right down to their friendships, their loves, their religious and political convictions."[9]

Corporate Takeover of Just About Everything

It is not just governments that seek to benefit from this huge expansion of emergency powers and emergency responses; so, too, do many large companies, particularly those in the tech sphere. Many of the world's biggest corporations, international banks, finance institutions, and billionaire-backed private foundations have been lobbying for and helping to implement digital immunity passports since even before the pandemic.

The Bill and Melinda Gates Foundation has influenced COVID-19 policies around the world, from facilitating the worldwide rollout of digital vaccine passports to intervening against the waiving of vaccine patent restrictions. Bill Gates himself has given countless interviews—often to media organizations his foundation helps fund—about COVID-19 and vaccines, despite having no medical qualifications to speak of. The Gates Foundation is the second largest donor to the World Health Organization (WHO), second only to the United States. So pervasive is the Foundation's influence over the policies adopted by the WHO that inside sources told *Politico* in 2017: "Gates' priorities have become the WHO's." Those priorities include spending a disproportionate amount of the WHO's resources on projects with the measurable outcomes Gates prefers, such as the effort to eradicate polio."[10]

The heavily conflicted Gates Foundation has invested billions in some of the world's biggest vaccine manufacturers including Pfizer and BioNTech. It is also a leading partner alongside Big Pharma in Gavi, the Vaccine Alliance, whose stated aim is to solve global health problems through vaccines. Both the Gates Foundation and Gavi have pushed the WHO to prioritize vaccine development and distribution above all other public health initiatives. It also recently helped finance a WHO paper providing "implementation guidance" for proof of vaccination certifications across the world. Also involved in the project was the Rockefeller Foundation and several high-level representatives of the World Bank.

Another institution pushing vaccine passports is the WEF. Best known for organizing the annual shindig of the global business, political, and cultural elite at Davos, Switzerland, the WEF is an NGO and think tank that claims to be "committed to improving the state of the world." In reality it is a hugely powerful global pressure group representing some of the world's wealthiest and most influential people and corporations that plays a leading role in shaping the global economy as well as social and environmental movements. As *Foreign Affairs* put it, "the WEF has no formal authority, but it has become the major forum for elites to discuss policy ideas and priorities."

In the early days of the COVID-19 pandemic, the WEF called for a "Great Reset," at the heart of which are WEF founder Klaus Schwab's concepts of the Fourth Industrial Revolution and stakeholder capitalism. In its essence, the Fourth Industrial Revolution (4IR) denotes the breakneck digital transformation we are currently living through, where just about everything becomes digitized, automated, and connected—all of it facilitated by big data. The 4IR will revolutionize the way people "live, work, and relate to one another," with implications "unlike anything humankind has experienced," says Schwab.[11]

The basic idea behind stakeholder capitalism is that the current model of global capitalism is no longer fit for purpose and should be reconfigured so that corporations no longer focus exclusively on serving shareholders but instead become custodians of society by creating value for all "stakeholders," including customers, suppliers, employees, and local communities. Under the new model a confluence of "multi-stakeholder partnerships" would bring together the private sector, governments, and civil society across all areas of global governance.

The idea sounds harmless enough—perhaps even desirable—until you realize that what it actually means is giving corporations even more power over society, at the expense of national democratic institutions. In the WEF's vision—laid out in its Global Redesign Initiative, drafted after the 2008 economic crisis—"the government voice would be one among many without always being the final arbiter." The question is: Who will be?

The ongoing global response to climate change may provide a few pointers. Despite playing a pivotal role in financing the world's biggest polluters for decades, some of the world's biggest banks and financial institutions are now writing the rules of "sustainable lending" for the future, warns a report jointly published by the Transnational Institute and Corporate Europe Observatory:

Since the agreement in Paris in late 2015, different constellations of financial corporations have worked to define methods for banks, investment funds, insurance companies and others to address the threat of a deeper climate crisis. Much of this work now, controversially, forms part of the official UN process. Not only this, but the corporations have been invited in not just to contribute to the event, but in fact to take over the implementation of the UN agenda on private finance and climate change. When the light is turned off and the doors are shut at the conclusion of COP26, the likes of BlackRock, Bank of America, Citigroup and Santander will take it from there . . .

[I]n some quarters there will be nods of appreciation when COP26 sees a parade of financial corporations committing to "net zero by 2050." Hundreds of financial institutions have signed up to UN-convened coalitions of companies promising to do their bit to fight climate change. But there are three serious problems with this approach: first, the commitments are so vague that they open the door to a potentially massive greenwash. Banks, asset managers and investment funds with massive holdings in fossil fuels and no concrete ambitions to change course can exploit the UN's programme to strengthen their image. Second, there is a risk that the presence of private finance in the overall architecture will be used by high-income

*countries to scale down their own financial commitments. Third,
the corporations are not only signing up to statements and making
commitments, they are in fact taking over the whole show.*[12]

A similar process is occurring with the roll out of vaccine passports.
The WEF, whose membership list reads like a Who's Who of the
world's biggest banks and corporations, wields significant influence
over the United Nations after signing a strategic partnership agreement
with the multilateral body in June 2019 aimed at "accelerat[ing] the
implementation of the 2030 Agenda for Sustainable Development."

From its inception the agreement sparked accusations of a corporate takeover of the UN's decision-making process. "[It] formalises
a disturbing corporate capture of the UN. It moves the world dangerously towards privatized and undemocratic global governance,"
said Gonzalo Berrón of Transnational Institute in presenting a letter
signed by 240 civil society organizations and 40 international networks. "The agreement gives transnational corporations preferential
and deferential access to the UN System at the expense of States and
public interest actors," warned the International Network for Economic, Social and Cultural Rights, which connects over 280 NGOs,
social movements, and advocates across more than 75 countries.[13]

The WEF has used its newfound clout at the UN to push the roll
out of both vaccine passports and digital IDs. It has even proposed
doing away with paper passports altogether, under the pretext of promoting mobility across nations.[14] In a white paper titled "Three Ways
to Accelerate a Digital-Led Recovery," the WEF argues that "to ignite
the spark of commercial and human progress, every person should
have a unique digital identity so that they have full access to the digital
world in the economic, social, and political realm." The white paper
even suggests that small and medium-sized businesses will benefit from
this development—a claim that could not be further from the truth.[15]

Killing Off Small Businesses

Small businesses have already borne the brunt of the economic
fallout from the COVID-19-induced lockdowns, slowdowns, and

work-from-home ordinances. As the white paper notes, these measures, applied in countries all over the world, have led "many in-person businesses to close their doors" while "helping digital-first businesses to grow." A lot of the small in-person businesses that remain standing took on huge amounts of debt to weather the lockdowns. Many of them are now struggling to repay that debt. According to research by the Bank of England (BoE), 33 percent of small businesses in the UK now have a high level of debt compared with 14 percent before COVID-19.

"Although debt appears affordable in the near term, insolvencies are likely to rise from 2021 Q4 as government support is withdrawn as planned," stated the BoE's Financial Policy Committee. Britain's employee furlough support program expired at the end of September, 2021, while the government's most generous support loans—part of the Bounce Back Loan Scheme—were phased out in March and replaced with the Recovery Loan Scheme.[16]

In China many small and micro businesses are also falling by the wayside as inflation fuels rising costs and the central government increasingly favors large state enterprises, according to a report by the *South China Morning Post*. There are roughly 139 million small businesses in China, according to one official tally. In China's official Purchasing Managers' Index in July 2021, many small and micro businesses complained of worsening conditions for the second straight month while large businesses said they saw slight growth.[17]

By their very nature, most small businesses depend heavily on local customers for their revenues, be they local people or other local businesses. They are the cornerstone of local communities, providing basic products and services, creating jobs, allowing local economies to flourish, and providing spaces and places for people to meet and engage with each other. Small and micro businesses are also essential to the health of the global economy. They make up the vast majority of businesses worldwide, representing around 90 percent of businesses and more than half of employment globally.

By essentially excluding unvaccinated people from small business premises, thus dramatically eroding their customer base, the vaccine passports will make it even harder for these businesses to survive. What's more, WEF hopes the vaccine passports will soon become digital IDs. All this will impose an extra layer of regulatory burdens and costs on small companies that do not have the resources and technical or legal know-how of large corporations.

In Scotland, business associations warned First Minister Nicola Sturgeon that her government's vaccine passport rules risked pushing already struggling companies over the cliff's edge. Liz Cameron, chief executive of the Scottish Chambers of Commerce, penned a letter to Sturgeon warning that firms "continue to operate in survival mode," adding that the "economic recovery is fragile and the long-term viability of many businesses and jobs remains in the balance."[18] The government stuck to its guns, becoming the first country in the United Kingdom to introduce vaccine passports.[19]

Representatives of the hospitality sector in Wales issued similar warnings about the Welsh Government's vaccine passport rules. "The news that COVID passports are to be required for entry into Welsh nightclubs and some large events from 11th October is incredibly disappointing," UKHospitality Executive Director for Wales David Chapman said. "This decision comes despite several weeks of meetings in which UKHospitality Cymru has repeatedly made the case against vaccine passports because of compliance difficulties over definitions of business, concerns over conflicts with customers, and a range of other implementational problems, all while the industry struggles to maintain viability and is trying to cope with desperately short staffing."[20]

Small businesses all over the world are facing a slew of supply chain headaches and labor issues. In the United States, 45 percent of small businesses were suffering domestic supplier delays in October 2021, up from 26.7 percent at the beginning of the year, according to the US Census Small Business Pulse Survey.[21] Supplies that small businesses depend upon are becoming harder to source, especially given that owners cannot always buy in bulk or in advance like larger companies. On top of that, a record 50 percent of the members of the National Federation of Independent Business (NFIB), the largest trade organization of small businesses, reported having job openings that couldn't be filled, up from 23 percent a year ago.

"Unfortunately, the challenge for small business owners is that the economy is breaking records in the wrong direction," said Bill G.

Smith, NFIB state director in Wisconsin. "A record 50 percent of our small business owners are reporting they are unable to fill job openings. That's a 48-year low. Another low is that small business optimism over the next six months has decreased to the lowest reading since 2012."[22]

Toward a New Economic Crisis?

It is against this backdrop that the US federal government decided in early November 2020 to expand its vaccine mandate to cover 80 million workers. President Biden announced that businesses with more than 100 workers on their payroll had until January 4 to ensure their workers are fully vaccinated, or tested weekly. If not, they could face federal fines starting at tens of thousands of dollars per offense.

Governments' vaccine passport policies also risk intensifying the centrifugal forces that have been crushing the global economy for the last year and a half. At a time when the world needs more workers than ever, governments and corporations are consigning millions of perfectly capable workers to the scrap heap for not taking a vaccine that does not prevent transmission of COVID-19 and only partially blocks infection.

Crucially, they include millions of workers in key strategic industries, such as shipping, logistics, transport, law enforcement, and health care. When Italy's government imposed its blanket "no jab, no job" mandate on October 15, 2021, 40 percent of the dockworkers at the country's most important commercial port, Trieste, were unvaccinated. Most of those workers refused to cave and began a weeks-long strike. The port became a focal point in Italy's anti–vaccine passport movement. After days of protests and blockages, the local police used force to evict the striking workers from the port. So they began gathering in Trieste's main square instead. But even that was not allowed. At the end of October, the local government banned all forms of protest in the main square until the end of the year, on the thin or specious grounds that the demonstrations had fueled a recent rise in COVID-19 infections.

Trieste's top law enforcement official, Valerio Valenti, said that the outbreak was "strictly correlated" to the antivaccine protests. "When balancing interests, in my opinion, the right to health prevails over the right to demonstrate."[23]

Other Italian cities, including Rome, Milan, and Bologna, have followed suit and cracked down on anti–Green Pass protests.[24]

But one thing authorities cannot do is force the port workers to work. And that is a problem given the importance of the port of Trieste to Europe's supply chains. Trieste is at the nexus of one of Europe's trade corridors, the Baltic–Adriatic Corridor, which is one of the most important trans-European road and railway axes in Central Europe. The longer the strike goes on, the more it threatens to exacerbate Europe's supply-chain crisis. The Draghi government's vaccine mandate also risks providing a huge boost to Italy's already large informal cash economy. Italy's Mafia families are no doubt rubbing their hands in glee, as unvaccinated workers are forced to work under the radar.

Given as much, the vaccine mandate should be seen as a huge, high-stakes bluff on the part of the Draghi government. If it pays off, the vast majority of Italy's vaccine holdouts will fall into line, take the vaccine, download the vaccine passport, and go back to work; and other governments across Europe will follow suit with similar "no jab, no job" mandates. But Draghi may have his work cut out given that vaccine cases in the country have done nothing but rise since the mandate was implemented. By the end of 2021 Italy was racking up 145,000 new cases per day—almost four times its previous record, registered in November 2020. If Draghi's ruse doesn't pay off and popular resistance rises, Italy's economy could be plunged into chaos and the Draghi government could be forced into an embarrassing retreat.

In the United States, the stakes are arguably even higher, given how important the country is to the global economy as well as the fact that it has more vaccine holdouts than most other Western countries. As in Italy, many logistics, transportation, and frontline workers refuse to relinquish their bodily autonomy. At the end of 2021 the United States was facing huge worker shortages despite the fact there were still 3.5 million fewer registered workers than two years prior.[25] Even before the mandate, the country already had a shortage of around 80,000 truckers. Jon Samson, an executive director at the American Trucking Associations, said that large trucking firms fear the mandate could trigger an exodus of workers to smaller firms or out of the industry altogether. The effect on America's already overstretched supply chains could be catastrophic.[26]

Other vital sectors are facing similar issues. Forty percent of the Transportation Security Administration's 50,000 agents remain unvaccinated. In October Southwest Airlines cancelled over 2,000 flights due to an alleged pilot "sick-out" over the company's vaccine mandate, although the company has denied this. Shortly after the cancellations the company's management softened its mandates policy, allowing unvaccinated workers to continue working as long as they seek exemption on medical or religious grounds. As Alex Gutentag writes in "Revolt of the Essential Workers", "Each local mandate battle ultimately contributes to a national high-stakes game of chicken that pits working people against a wealthy, increasingly authoritarian overclass."

While all this is happening, the disconnect between the real economy and the financial markets has never been greater. Although the world witnessed a massive surge in pent-up demand during the first six months of 2021, the recovery had already begun to fizzle out by the third quarter. The US economy grew at an annualized rate of only 2 percent in Q3—the slowest rate of economic growth since the start of the recovery. The highly infectious Delta variant, supply-chain chaos, worker shortages, rising inflation, and the fading effects of the stimulus sugar rush were all weighing on economic activity.

At a global level the economic impact of last year's lockdowns and slowdowns continues to mount. By late October poverty, inequality, and unemployment were bigger concerns than the coronavirus pandemic, according to an Ipsos MORI poll of twenty-eight countries. Sixty-four percent of the survey's respondents said they thought their country was heading in the wrong direction.[27] Much of the data suggests we are in the early stages of economic collapse. Many of the causes of the last economic crisis—including the huge levels of private debt (much of which was shifted onto public ledgers), unfettered speculation in the financial markets, and the creation of ever-more destructive financial instruments—were never properly addressed. Most of the policy choices of governments and central banks have merely served to exacerbate economic risks and inequality.

A crisis is already brewing in China, the world's second largest economy that almost single-handedly lifted the global economy out of the last financial crisis. The Chinese government's decision to reduce the economy's reliance on real estate, while certainly salient, is fraught with risks. In a worst-case scenario it could spark a disorderly collapse of the world's biggest property market. By late summer 2021, local governments were scrambling to launch rescue funds worth billions of dollars to bail out state-owned groups after a flurry of defaults. In August, China Huarong Asset Management received a $16 billion rescue package. But government support has been less forthcoming for other struggling borrowers, including property developers. On December 10, China Evergrande Group, the world's most debt-saddled property developer, entered default, while many smaller Chinese real estate developers teetered on the edge.

As Bloomberg reported on January 2, 2022, "China's property developers have mounting bills to pay and shrinking options to raise necessary funds." In January alone, "the industry will need to find at least $197 billion to cover maturing bonds, coupons, trust products and deferred wages to millions of migrant workers, according to Bloomberg calculations and analyst estimates."[28] Smaller construction companies in particular are struggling to find funding. If fallout from Evergrande's default is not contained, it could spark another global financial crisis.

Yet investors in the West remain sanguine. Financial markets on both sides of the Atlantic were still hitting record highs on a regular basis. By November 1, 2021, the S&P 500 had registered more than 50 new highs in 2021 alone and the Nasdaq was over 80 percent higher than its pre-pandemic level. By the end of the year, the S&P 500, the Nasdaq Composite Index, the FTSE 100, Germany's DAX 30, and France's CAC 40 were all at or near record highs.

One obvious reason for this is that many of the world's biggest publicly listed banks and corporations, awash with stimulus money, were once again buying back their own shares rather than investing in new products, machinery, or workers. This is a great way to enrich shareholders but is a net negative for the overall economy, since all it does is further inflate asset prices, enriching the 10 percent of the population that owns most financial assets, while creating no new products or services. Not so long ago, share buybacks were deemed a form of market manipulation and were banned under US Securities and Exchange Commission (SEC) rules. Then in 1982 the SEC issued Rule 10b-18, which provided corporations a "safe harbor" to buy back their own shares under certain conditions. Since then, the practice has exploded. As the San Francisco-based financial analyst Wolf Richter reported in March 2020, S&P 500 companies squandered $4.5 trillion on share buybacks between 2012 and 2020.[29] In 2021, both Apple and Microsoft executed their biggest ever share buybacks, propelling their stock to even greater highs.

But record stock valuations are normally a sign that a correction is probably in order. By the end of 2021, the bottom lines of even the world's biggest companies, including Amazon, were beginning to feel the effects of rising inflation, surging global labor costs and operational disruptions. Financial risks were once again on the rise. To respond to rising inflation, many central banks have begun hiking interest rates and tapering their quantitative easing (QE) programs. The Federal Reserve has signaled that it will do the same in early 2022. A sudden tightening of central bank monetary policy around the world, while almost certainly necessary to contain inflation, is likely to trigger a sharp correction in stock and bond markets, as already happened in late 2018. It will also probably lead to a stronger dollar, heaping even more pressure on emerging market currencies and economies.

After little more than a year, the global economic recovery is fizzling at the same time that inequality, poverty, and unemployment are weighing on the minds and pockets of the billions of people who can't afford to buy Apple and Microsoft shares. When this boom turns to bust, leaving even more unemployment and inequality in its wake, those people are going to be desperate and angry. Many will even be hungry. If 2019 was the year of protest, 2022 could be the year of unbottled rage. But before that happens, governments and global corporations are determined to rush into existence vaccine passport and digital ID systems that provide them much greater control of the world's restive populations.

CHAPTER SIX

A New Social Contract

"Now this is not the end. It is not even the beginning of the end. But it is, perhaps, the end of the beginning."

These immortal words belong, of course, to Winston Churchill. They were said on November 10, 1942, after Alexander and Montgomery had turned back Rommel's forces at El Alamein, thereby winning what Churchill called "The Battle of Egypt." In February 2021, a little-known organization called the Good Health Pass Collaborative (goodhealthpass.org) borrowed Churchill's words for its promotional document, "A Safe Guide to Global Reopening." The words featured as a pull quote in a section titled "Opportunities and Challenges," which is apt considering that is precisely what vaccine passports represent to many of the companies, governments, and supranational organizations rolling them out: a historic opportunity as well as a challenge.

For the Good Health Pass initiative, the most important challenge is ensuring that the myriad vaccine passport systems are interoperable:

> *Because numerous companies around the world are racing to market with digital health credential solutions, it is unlikely that one solution will be implemented globally. Thus, it is vitally important that solutions are designed for interoperability—both with one another and across institutional and geographic borders. This can only be achieved through a set of open standards to which all digital health pass systems must adhere. Failing to address interoperability could undermine acceptance, adoption, and ultimately, the utility of digital health passes.* [1]

The Good Health Pass Collaborative's members include an assortment of vaccine passport developers as well as global corporations and institutions, such as Mastercard, IBM, Airports Council International, the Grameen Foundation, and the International Chamber of Commerce. The initiative was the brainchild of ID2020, an obscure New York–based nonprofit that describes itself as "a global alliance for ethical, privacy-protecting approaches to digital IDs." The ID2020 Alliance was not set up in 2020 but in 2016, with seed money from Microsoft, Accenture, PricewaterhouseCoopers, the Rockefeller Foundation, Cisco, and Gavi, the Vaccine Alliance, which itself was cofounded by the Bill and Melinda Gates Foundation and is financially supported by many of the world's biggest companies and the governments of the world's wealthiest countries.[2]

ID2020's founding mission is to provide digital identities for *all people*, including the world's most vulnerable populations by 2030. At its inaugural summit, representatives of tech companies, such as Microsoft and Accenture, as well as UN agencies, such as the World Food Programme, waxed lyrical about creating a digital ID tied to fingerprints, birth date, medical records, education, travel, bank accounts, and more. And the gateway for achieving that goal is vaccination.

Vaccine Passport = Digital ID

The vaccine passport is nothing more and nothing less than a digital ID. Since at least 2016 a powerful alliance of UN agencies, global corporations, and wealthy foundations has set its sights on creating and implementing digital ID around the world. Organizations such as ID2020, the Good Health Pass Collaborative, the Vaccine Credential Initiative, the CommonPass, and Gavi are the vehicles by which they hope to achieve that goal. The COVID-19 pandemic and the subsequent roll out of novel vaccine technologies have provided the pretext.

In March 2018, almost two full years before the coronavirus pandemic, ID2020 published an article titled "Immunization: An Entry Point for Digital Identity." The article stated that "immunization poses a huge opportunity to scale digital identity":

[I]n many developing countries, immunization coverage greatly exceeds birth registration rates. According to best available estimates, upwards of 95% of children globally receive at least one dose of one vaccine (with 86% of children globally receiving the full three doses recommended of the diphtheria-tetanus-pertussis vaccine, which is commonly used to measure immunization coverage).

When a child receives her first vaccine, she receives a paper child health card. In many developing countries, the most common form of identification is not a birth certificate, but this card. The near ubiquity of these documents presents an enormous opportunity. [3]

That opportunity could not be clearer: to use global health challenges as a pretext for implementing digital identity programs around the world, which is precisely what is happening right now.

While digital identity may offer certain benefits for citizens, including greater ease in verifying one's identity as well as the convenience of having all your digital records stored in one place, it also poses huge dangers. The biggest danger of all is that governments and companies will have much greater ability to track and control populations, impose behaviors, and influence politics. The worldwide roll out of vaccine passports/digital IDs represents nothing less than the redrawing of the social contract—a fact the World Economic Forum admitted in its 2018 report, "Identity in a Digital World: A New Chapter in the Social Contract":

Government, private-sector and civil society communities from the World Economic Forum network have identified six priority areas for collaboration to help shape digital identities of the future:

1. *Moving the emphasis beyond identity for all to identities that deliver user value*
2. *Creating metrics and accountability for good identity*
3. *Building new governance models for digital identity ecosystems*
4. *Promoting stewardship of good identity*
5. *Encouraging partnerships around best practices and interoperability where appropriate*

6. Innovating with technologies and models and building a library of successful pilots

As the International Organization for Public-Private Cooperation, the World Economic Forum offers a platform for such collaboration that advances the practice of "good" identities and maximizes value to individuals.[4]

At the WEF's Annual Meeting in Davos 2018, senior representatives of business, governments, and civil society made a commitment to advance towards a "good" future for digital identity. In the months following, those stakeholders identified an initial set of five requirements that a "good" identity should satisfy, which the WEF shared in its "Identity in a Digital World" report. For a digital ID to be good, it must:

1. Be fit for purpose, by offering "a reliable way for individuals to build trust in who they claim to be, to exercise their rights and freedoms and/or in their eligibility to carry out digital interactions";
2. Be secure—protecting individuals, organizations, devices, and infrastructure from identity theft, unauthorized data sharing, and human rights violations.
3. Be useful, meaning it "offers access to a wide range of useful services and interactions and is easy to establish and use."
4. Offer choice. A digital ID can be empowering for users, the report claims, allowing them to control "what data they share for which interaction, with whom, and for how long." This is most likely an empty promise. After all, how much control and ownership do we have over the reams of digital data we generate today?
5. Be inclusive. This is a popular buzzword, often used to describe things that are anything but. For example, the cashless economy is often marketed as a means of promoting "financial inclusion," when it does the exact opposite. Those who stand to benefit most from a cashless economy are in the more comfortable classes, who by and large are computer literate and already use digital money for most of their transactions, while those

most dependent on cash—the poor and the elderly—will suddenly find life a lot more difficult.

So, who would benefit most from a system of mandatory digital IDs? The most likely answer to that question is the WEF's most important stakeholders: the world's most powerful corporations, biggest financial institutions, and wealthiest individuals. In others words, Davos Man and Davos Woman.

Recall from chapter 4 (see "Corporate Takeover of Just about Everything") that in 2019 the WEF pulled off the mother of all public-private partnerships when it signed a strategic partnership agreement with the United Nations, granting multinational corporations even more influence over global governance in the name of accelerating the implementation of the 2030 Agenda for Sustainable Development. The strategic partnership agreement represented a seismic shift in the UN's founding commitment from multilateralism to the WEF's model of multi-stakeholderism, gifting corporations a preferential place within the UN system.

When it comes to shaping the global agenda, the WEF is also able to lever its vast network of business owners and senior business executives, politicians, scientists, journalists, and other opinion makers, as well as leaders of global institutions. Its board of trustees includes Kristalina Georgieva, the managing director of the International Monetary Fund; Larry Fink, the CEO of BlackRock, the world's biggest fund manager, which wields huge influence over policy at the US Federal Reserve and other key central banks; Christine Lagarde, the president of the European Central Bank; Jack Ma, the cofounder and former executive chairman of the Chinese tech giant Alibaba Group; Mark Carney, the former governor of the Bank of England, who is now (in the words of the *Wall Street Journal*) the "UN's point man on global climate finance"[5]; and former US Vice President Al Gore.

Since 1993 the WEF has been running the Global Leaders for Tomorrow program, which now goes by the name of the Forum of Young Global Leaders. To qualify for membership, you must be younger than 38 years old and highly accomplished in your respective field. In 2008 Businessweek's Bruce Nussbaum described the

Forum of Young Global Leaders as "the most exclusive private social network in the world." The organization itself says its members represent "the voice for the future and the hopes of the next generation."

The program's organizers certainly have a knack of picking future global leaders. Now in its 29th year, the program has well over a thousand current members and alumni. They include many Silicon Valley billionaires, from Bill Gates (Microsoft) to Mark Zuckerberg (Facebook), to Peter Thiel (Palantir), to Jeff Bezos (Amazon), to Pierre Omidyar (eBay), to Eric Schmidt (Google) and Larry Page (Google). They also include many heads of state and health ministers, current and former, who have wielded a huge amount of influence over their respective country's COVID-19 response, particularly in Europe. Here are a few examples:

- Former UK Prime Minister and vaccine passport champion Tony Blair
- Former UK Prime Minister and Chancellor of the Exchequer Gordon Brown
- Former German Chancellor Angela Merkel, who dominated German politics between 2005 and 2021
- Former President of the European Commission Jean-Claude Juncker
- French President Emmanuel Macron
- German Health Minister Jens Spahn
- Former taoiseach of Ireland (2017–2020) Leo Varadkar
- Sanna Marin, the prime minister of Finland
- Sebastian Kurz, the former chancellor of Austria (initially from December 2017 to May 2019 and then a second time from January 2020 to October 2021)
- Alexander De Croo, the current prime minister of Belgium
- Jacinda Ardern, the prime minister of New Zealand[6]

A New Social Contract

In the new social contract envisioned by the WEF and laid out in its 2018 report, "Identity in a Digital World," corporations and governments will have total, seamless control over citizens' lives. Take, for instance, the EU's vaccine certificate—the so-called Green Pass—which has been in gestation since 2018, over a year before the COVID-19 pandemic began.[7] The goal was to have a common vaccination card/passport for all EU citizens in place by 2022 as well as make EU Member States' national immunization information systems interoperable. Thanks to the catalytic role of the COVID-19 pandemic, those objectives were already achieved by 2021. Rather than setting you free, the Green Pass ties you inexorably to the whims of government and corporations. Without the Green Pass, Italian citizens cannot work, at least not within the confines of the official economy. In some countries, you cannot access most public services or study without it.

It is a system of exclusion rather than inclusion. As the WEF itself admits, while verifiable identities "create new markets and business lines" for companies, especially those in the tech industry that will help to operate the ID systems while no doubt hoovering up the data, they (emphasis my own) "open up (*or close off*) the digital world" for individuals. This is the new social contract the WEF wants to create. As I'll cover in chapter 7, it shares some of the trappings of the hugely ambitious social credit system under construction in China. As in China, many of the administrative decisions that control our lives will be made by machines rather than people.

This degree of surveillance and control should disturb us, even if the technology were to operate perfectly. But, as we know, technology doesn't operate perfectly. Mistakes or biases introduced into algorithms could have profound effects on individual lives and society-wide, possibly becoming more pronounced and entrenched over time. Consider this: between 2015 and 2018 Amazon tried to eradicate gender bias in its AI-based hiring practices, but couldn't, and ended up having to give up.[8] If Amazon can't eliminate bias in its AI programming, who can?

But the WEF is still determined to push digital IDs into existence, just about everywhere. At its 2018 Annual Meeting in Davos, attendees—including representatives of the world's biggest banks, tech firms, and multinational corporations—"committed to shared cooperation on advancing good, user-centric digital identities. Since then, a broader group of stakeholders has joined this conversation: experts, policy-makers, business executives, practitioners, rights advocates, humanitarian organizations and civil society."[9]

In other words, almost two years before the COVID-19 pandemic even began, many of the world's most powerful companies and institutions had already agreed to create and install digital ID systems around the world. This vision is now unfolding before our eyes. The technologies already exist to make it happen. On its corporate website, the IT services and consulting firm Accenture, which helped set up ID2020, states that it has already developed a Unique Identity Service Platform "to deploy a breakthrough biometrics system that can manage fingerprints, iris scans, and other data."[10]

The system forms part of the ID2020 Alliance's plan to "provide a global identity solution," Accenture says. "The alliance draws on advances in biometrics and innovative technologies and brings together expertise from business, government, and nongovernment agencies. Our experts at the Dublin Innovation Center contribute cross-functional and cross-cultural expertise to drive it forward in collaboration with both UN and other global humanitarian organizations."

In September 2019, just months before the COVID-19 outbreak in Wuhan, China, ID2020 began putting some of its ideas into practice. Through a partnership agreement with Gavi (the global Vaccine Alliance) and the government of Bangladesh, ID2020 launched what it called "a good digital identity program" (the same language used by the WEF) for the newborn infants of Bangladesh. Seizing on the opportunity for immunization to serve as a platform for digital identity, the program leveraged existing vaccination and birth registration operations to offer newborns a biometrically-linked digital identity.

"We are implementing a forward-looking approach to digital identity that gives individuals control over their own personal information, while still building off existing systems and programs," said Anir Chowdhury, policy advisor at the Access to Information (a2i) Program of the Government of Bangladesh. "The Government of Bangladesh recognizes that the design of digital identity systems carries far-reaching implications for individuals' access to services and livelihoods, and we are eager to pioneer this approach."

Dakota Gruener, executive director of ID2020 (and a former employee of Gavi, the Vaccine Alliance), was also thrilled by the initiative:

> *Digital ID is being defined and implemented today, and we recognize the importance of swift action to close the identity gap. Now is the time for bold commitments to ensure that we respond both quickly and responsibly. We and our ID2020 Alliance partners, both present and future, are committed to rising to this challenge.* [11]

Once the COVID-19 pandemic had begun, it didn't take long for ID2020's members to shift the conversation to digital identity. The Rockefeller Foundation wrote in April 2020 in the position paper "National COVID-19 Testing Action Plan," published just weeks into the pandemic:

> *Those screened must be given a unique patient identification number that would link to information about a patient's viral, antibody and eventually vaccine status under a system that could easily handshake with other systems to speed the return of normal societal functions. Schools could link this to attendance lists, large office buildings to employee ID cards, TSA to passenger lists and concert and sports venues to ticket purchasers.* [12]

Many of the world's most advanced economies, particularly in Europe, have already adopted some of the foundation's suggestions. In poorer parts of the world, where vaccine take-up is lower, digital IDs are being pushed through on wholly different pretexts. In Mexico, the government is on the verge of establishing a mandatory biometric ID system, with $250 million of funds provided by the World Bank's Identification for Development (ID4D) program. Launched in 2014 with "catalytic contributions" from the Gates Foundation, the Omidyar Network, and the governments of the UK, France, and Australia, the program is a "cross-sectoral platform that creates and leverages partnerships with United Nations agencies, other donors, nongovernment organizations, academia, and the private sector" with the goal of "help[ing] countries realize the transformational potential of digital identification systems."[13]

The European Commission is also pushing countries in its outer orbit that provide large inflows of migration into the EU, mainly in Africa, the Middle East, and non-EU member states in the Balkans, including some countries with egregious human rights records, to set up biometric databases, reports London-based charity Privacy International. In some cases, such as Nigeria, the Commission has partnered with the World Bank to provide financing for the development of the digital ID systems.[14]

As these systems are put into place through the rollout of vaccine passports and other forms of digital ID, the citizens of the world should be deeply concerned, for three main reasons. First, the vaccine passports will deliver the final fatal blow to personal privacy. Second, they will provide governments, companies, and other state and nonstate actors with access to our most precious data of all: our health and biometric data. And third is the risk of mission creep: while advertised as digital vaccination records, vaccine passports are clearly intended to be used for much, much more.

The End of All Privacy

Vaccine passports raise huge privacy concerns. Data-hungry companies like Microsoft, a member of the Vaccine Credential Initiative; Facebook; and Google's parent company Alphabet, which is invested in new vaccine technologies, will be given fresh opportunities to track our daily movements and activities and share those data with third parties. This is how they make much of their money. As the German financial journalist Norbert Häring warns, the mad rush to roll out vaccine passports threatens to enshrine Silicon Valley tech giants—which have already amassed far too much monopoly power at the public's expense, including the power to censor information on the internet—as global passport authorities.

Everyday citizens have already sacrificed much of their privacy in exchange for the ability to navigate the internet and use social media. We thought we were getting a fair deal. To use the services of tech giants like Google, Facebook, and Twitter free of charge, all we had to do was let those companies exploit our personal data, which they repackaged and sold to support targeted, personalized advertising. This is the basis of what Professor Carissa Véliz of the Institute for Ethics in AI at the University of Oxford calls the *data economy*. The price we ended up paying was our own personal privacy. As Véliz says, privacy is important because it protects us from the influence of others.[15]

> *The more companies know about you, the more power they have over you. If they know you are desperate for money, they will take advantage of your situation and show you ads for abusive payday loans. If they know your race, they may not show you ads for certain exclusive places or services, and you would never know that you were discriminated against. If they know what tempts you, they will design products to keep you hooked, even if that can damage your health, hurt your work, or take time away from your family or from basic needs like sleep. If they know what your fears are, they will use them to lie to you about politics and manipulate you into voting for their preferred candidate. Foreign countries use data about our personalities to polarize us in an effort to undermine public trust and cooperation. The list goes on and on.*

Even people who go out of their way to protect their personal data and privacy from the roving eyes of Big Tech still end up getting caught in their data dragnet. As the sociologist and *New York Times* columnist Zeynep Tufekci has noted, the power of Big Data means that even if you strive to protect your privacy, online companies such as Facebook can now infer "a wide range of things about you that you may have never disclosed, including your moods, your political beliefs, your sexual orientation, and your health."[16]

The arrival of vaccine passports / digital IDs will enable both companies and governments unprecedented access to some of our most personal—and valuable—data of all: our health data. That data is of immense value to all kinds of companies, particularly pharmaceuticals and insurance companies.

Our current data economy is based on collecting as much personal data as possible, storing it indefinitely, and selling it to the highest bidder, says Véliz. "Having so much sensitive data circulating freely is reckless."

Most governments, tech giants, banks, and other companies have already shown they cannot be trusted with our data. The data they accumulate about us is often shared, usually at a price and often without our consent, with third-party companies, governments, police authorities, or even security services. Even governments that have gone out of their way to protect health data, such as Finland, have faced privacy problems.[17]

In Canada, Ontario's former privacy commissioner, Ann Cavoukian, warned in October 2021 that the government's vaccine passport system would create a highly intrusive surveillance system that not only compels Canadians to reveal their health information but can also track their movements. Two months later, she sounded the alarm again about the government's tracking of cellphone data to inform its pandemic response, after it emerged that the Public Health Agency of Canada (PHAC) has been covertly analyzing the movements of Canadians since the onset of the pandemic.

"In March 2020, [Prime Minister Justin] Trudeau said that tracking cellphone users was not being considered. Well, they did it, PHAC's been doing it, and they want to do it even more," said Cavoukian, adding: "It concerns me enormously that this would enable the government to collect more and more information. I do not want to [see] a trend where the government is consistently doing this and starting now. You can't trust the government."[18] In mid-January 2022, it emerged that German authorities had unlawfully acquired encrypted data from a COVID-19 contact tracing app to track down witnesses in a criminal investigation. As the German international broadcaster *Deutsche Welle* reported, the case exemplifies concerns voiced by data protection experts.[19]

In urgent need of cash, the UK's National Health Service recently decided to digitize and sell off the private health data of all 55 million of its users to private companies and other third parties. "One of the great requirements for health tech is a single health database," Damindu Jayaweera, head of technology research at Peel Hunt, told

Investors' Chronicle. "There are only two places as far as I know that digitise the data of the whole population from birth to death . . . China and the UK."[20]

Of course, that data for sale included highly sensitive information on physical, mental, and sexual health, as well as gender, ethnicity, criminal records, and history of abuse—information that NHS patients give in confidence to their general practitioner. NHS Digital executives would allow people, in theory, to opt out of the scheme, except they failed to announce that the scheme even existed until right before the opt-out deadline passed.

When the *Financial Times* ran an exposé in May 2021, NHS Digital was forced to shelve the scheme.[21] Unfortunately, NHS Digital had already begun sharing patient data with over 40 global companies, including McKinsey & Company, KPMG, Experian, and a big data firm cofounded by the Sackler family, whose drug company, Purdue Pharma, was one of the main instigators behind the US opioid crisis.[22] NHS Digital also shared patient data with the scandal-tarnished US spytech firm Palantir, which provides data-science support to US military operations, mass surveillance, and predictive policing. Perhaps most controversial of all, despite claims of confidentiality, NHS Digital ended up sharing the health data of more than 80 percent of the NHS patients who chose to opt out of the data-sharing program. The *FT* "found that insights from the data were often shared or sold on to other commercial entities and providers that use it to price products being sold back to the NHS, or conversely restrict the NHS's access to analysis of its own data, creating conflicts of interest. Among the biggest criticisms focused on the opacity around the data's fate after it leaves the NHS's servers, and the lack of an auditing trail beyond the companies on the register."[23]

Unfortunately, the scandal doesn't appear to have prompted much in the way of meaningful change at NHS Digital. Within three months, another scandal erupted, this time revolving around facial recognition data collected by the NHS App, a multifaceted platform that can be used by NHS patients to access the NHS certificate proving their COVID-19 vaccination status. But to access the App, NHS patients must share their facial recognition data—data that's being managed by undisclosed companies. Worse still, the NHS appears to be sharing some of that facial recognition data with law enforcement agencies, according to *The Guardian*. It is also likely to be of interest to UK and foreign intelligence services.[24]

With more and more companies and government agencies getting their hands on our health data, the security of that data is becoming increasingly precarious. If recent history has taught us anything, it is that no data is completely secure. And that should be a major cause for concern given that many vaccine certificates are likely to include our most precious data of all: our biometric data.

Biometrics: The Most Precious Data of All

Biometrics systems are used to identify or authenticate identity by using innate physical or behavioral characteristics, including fingerprints, face and palm prints, iris patterns, voice, gait, breath, and DNA. The argument for its use is that by tying digital IDs to biometrics, authorities can largely remove the risk of fraud and identity theft, an issue that's recently come up with vaccine passports in France and elsewhere.

Biometric technologies are already being used in diverse settings, from banks and other financial institutions to schools and workplaces. UK global bank Standard Chartered has rolled out fingerprint and other biometric technologies across many of the African and Asian markets in which it operates, as part of a $1.5 billion technology investment package. Mexican banks have collected biometric data (fingerprints and iris scans) on all their customers. Passports around the world have included biometric features for years, as have other forms of IDs. Many people opt to sign into their mobile phones using their biometric data.

Children are also being conditioned to use biometric systems, sometimes for the most mundane of reasons. In Scotland, for example, a number of schools in 2021 began using facial recognition to expedite school lunch lines. The local council in North Ayrshire said that the new technology allowed for a faster lunch service while removing the need for any contact at the point of sale: "With Facial Recognition, pupils simply select their meal, look at the camera and go, making for a faster lunch service whilst removing any contact at the point of sale."[25]

Similar facial recognition systems have been in use in the United States for years, though usually as a security measure. In the case of the schools in Ayrshire, the rationale is ease, speed, and efficiency, but critics argue that these pilot schemes have a much darker purpose than expediting school lunch queues; they are about conditioning children to the widespread use of facial recognition and other biometric technologies.

Stephanie Hare, author of *Technology Ethics*, argues that the widespread use of these technologies is normalizing children to understand "their bodies as something they use to transact. That's how you condition an entire society to use facial recognition."

In the end, North Ayrshire council decided to shelve its pilot scheme after parents and data ethics experts raised concerns that the privacy implications may not have been fully considered.[26] There has also been pushback from citizens in the United States on the use of facial recognition in schools. In New York, public opposition was so strong that the state government ended up halting all use of biometric identifying technology in schools until at least July 2022.

San Francisco-based digital rights group Electronic Frontier Foundation says that biometric systems pose "extreme risks" to privacy and the security of personal data:

> *The government insists that biometrics databases can be used effectively for border security, to verify employment, to identify criminals, and to combat terrorism. Private companies argue biometrics can enhance our lives by helping us to identify our friends more easily and by allowing us access to places, products, and services more quickly and accurately. But the privacy risks that accompany biometrics databases are extreme.*
>
> *Biometrics' biggest risk to privacy comes from the government's ability to use it for surveillance. As face recognition technologies become more effective and cameras are capable of recording greater and greater detail, surreptitious identification and tracking could become the norm.*

The problems are multiplied when biometrics databases are "multimodal," allowing the collection and storage of several different biometrics in one database and combining them with traditional data points like name, address, social security number, gender, race, and date of birth. Further, geolocation tracking technologies built on top of large biometrics collections could enable constant surveillance.[27]

This is a problem highlighted in a *Financial Times* article about Aadhaar, India's biometric ID system. It came into being in 2016 after the government passed the Aadhaar Act without any debate, discussion, or even the approval of Parliament. Aadhaar (Hindi for "foundation") is a 12-digit unique identity number (UID) issued by the government after confirming a person's biometric and demographic information. The largest system of its kind on the planet, Aadhaar required Indian citizens to submit their photograph, iris, and fingerprint scans in order to qualify for welfare benefits, compensation, scholarships, legal entitlements, and even nutrition programs. By 2021, the Unique Identification Authority of India (UIDAI) had issued 1.3 billion UIDs covering roughly 92 percent of the population.

The UIDAI was led by Indian tech billionaire Nandan Nilekani, the cofounder and nonexecutive chairman of Infosys, India's second largest IT company. Lauded by Bill Gates as one of his so-called "heroes in the field" for having made the world's "invisible people, visible," Nilekani has in recent years been working with the World Bank to help other governments set up similar digital ID systems.[28]

Besides serving as a gateway to government services, Aadhaar also tracks users' movements between cities, their employment status, and purchasing records. It is a de facto social credit system that serves as the key entry point for accessing services in India. While the system has helped to speed and clean up India's bureaucracy, it has also massively increased the Indian government's surveillance powers and excluded over 100 million people from welfare programs as well as basic services, as the *FT* article notes:

The Indian media has reported several cases of cardless individuals starving to death because they could not access benefits to which they were entitled. "Aadhaar is deeply embedded in Indian life and works for most people most of the time. However, when it does not work, it most affects those who are already vulnerable," the [2019 State of Aadhaar] report concluded.

Some critics go further, arguing Aadhaar has largely failed to fulfil its original promise of improving welfare and now acts as a tool for social exclusion and corporate influence. In Dissent on Aadhaar *(2019), 15 academics, lawyers and technologists examined Aadhaar's shortcomings, focusing on an almost Kafkaesque disparity between the "helplessness, frustration and vulnerability" of the individual and the omniscience and opacity of large bureaucracies. "The Aadhaar project is a perversion of the constructive purpose of technology to be subservient to the needs of society," concluded Reetika Khera, the book's lead author.* [29]

Biometric systems are also prone to failure, warns the London-based charity Privacy International:

This can be a result of issues like the fading of fingerprints (the elderly and manual workers being particularly at risk) or cataracts affecting iris scans.

The consequences of this can be severe: for example, failing to get access to benefits to which an individual is entitled. This is not an abstract concern. There are already reports that this has led to starvation deaths in India. [30]

The systems are also notoriously inaccurate on women and those with darker skin, and they may also be inaccurate on children whose facial characteristics change rapidly. *Wired* magazine reported in 2019 that "US government tests find even top-performing facial recognition systems misidentify blacks at rates five to 10 times higher than they do whites." [31]

There is also the risk that people's biometric identifiers could end up in the wrong hands. A large-scale data breech in India, for example, could affect over a billion people. Privacy International reports that authorities in India, South Korea, and the Philippines have already suffered "extensive security and data breaches that led to the leaking of biometric ID information belonging to millions of individuals in those respective countries." If biometric data is hacked, there is no way of undoing the damage. You cannot change or cancel your iris, fingerprint, or DNA like you can change a password or cancel your credit card.

"The idea of a data breach is not a question of if, it's a question of when," says Professor Sandra Wachter, a data ethics expert at the Oxford Internet Institute. "Welcome to the internet: everything is hackable."

Most databases are exceedingly porous, even in countries with advanced cybersecurity systems, as we saw in the recent hack of Microsoft's exchange servers.[32] Governmental databases are often targets because they have fewer resources and often less skilled IT teams.[33] Central banks, such as the Reserve Bank of New Zealand and Banco de Mexico, have also been targeted by cybercriminals. These incidents raise concerns about any system that seeks to collect, integrate, and use the biometric identifiers of hundreds of millions or even billions of people. While most vaccine passport systems haven't collected users' biometric data yet, it is probably a matter of time before they do. That data is unlikely to be fully secure.

Peter Yapp, former deputy director of UK Government Communications Headquarters's (GCHQ's) National Cyber Security Centre (NCSC) recently warned that building another centralized database to store even more of our personal data would create more opportunities for hackers and cybercriminals:

> *Centralised databases mean you're putting a lot of data in one place so it becomes an attractive target for hackers and the like, so it's like a honeypot—it attracts people in and they're going to have a go because there is so much data.*

Steve Baker, deputy leader of the COVID Recovery Group (CRG) of Conservative MPs, said a centralized vaccine passport system would become a magnet for hackers:

Bugs create security vulnerabilities. That's why it's a terrible idea to gather together so much data of such importance in one place. This is one more nail in the coffin in the idea of COVID certification. [34]

There is another reason why vaccine passport systems are a threat to our personal liberties, privacy, and digital rights: that the scale and scope of their application will grow over time.

Mission Creep

When the European Union launched its Green Pass initiative in June 2021, it was supposedly intended to reopen the bloc's borders and make international tourism possible once again. But within months it was being used by many Member States to exclude unvaccinated people from accessing many public spaces and basic services. Italy's government has used its iteration of the Green Pass to effectively ban almost four million people from being able to earn a living. In Austria the government locked down around two million people for not being vaccinated, before relenting five days later and locking down everyone else.

This has happened despite the fact that the EU's own Green Pass legislation stipulates that "[t]he issuance of [COVID] certificates . . . should not lead to discrimination on the basis of the possession of a specific category of certificate."[35] The Council of Europe, Europe's pre-eminent human rights organization, went even further, arguing not only that no one should be "discriminated against for not having been vaccinated" but also that the vaccination should not be mandatory.[36]

To complement its Green Pass, the EU has already launched a digital wallet that will be used to store peoples' surnames, first names, dates and place of birth, gender or nationality, as well as enable Europeans to identify themselves online. This is part and parcel of the digital identity revolution being spearheaded by organizations like the World Economic Forum, Gavi, and ID2020.

In a similar vein, the UK government quietly announced on December 27, 2021, just weeks after introducing its vaccine passport system, plans to develop a "digital identity and attributes trust framework" that will "enable employers and landlords (letting agents) to use certified identification document validation technology (IDVT) service providers to carry out digital identity checks on their behalf for many who are not in scope to use the Home Office online services, including British and Irish citizens, from 6 April 2022."[37]

Once vaccine passport/digital ID systems are established, mission creep is virtually guaranteed. But don't take my word for it; the French defense contractor Thales Group laid it out in an internal blog authored by its head of digital identity services portfolio, Kristel Teyras:

> *The ambition is huge; both in terms of scale—as it applies to all EU member states—and also in the power it would grant to citizens throughout the Bloc. For the first time, citizens would be able to use a European Digital Identity wallet, from their phone, that would give them access to services in any region across Europe.* [38]

Note Teyras's use of the verb "would be able to" in the second sentence. As German finance journalist Norbert Häring points out, "if we want to remove the gloss . . . we would only have to replace 'be able to' with 'have to.'"

"That sounds a bit scarier, doesn't it?" asks Häring.

One of the companies involved in the development of the UK's COVID-19 vaccine passport, the US IT firm Entrust, said that the vaccine passport system could also be "redeployed" as a national ID card. This is despite the fact that a previous digital ID card scheme was scrapped in 2011 following a public outcry against the intrusion and potential for human rights violations it would entail.

In a blog written shortly before Entrust was awarded a £250,000 contract in May 2021 to provide the cloud software for the UK's vaccine certification system, the company's product marketing manager Jenn Markey noted that:

> *Vaccine credentials can become part of the infrastructure of the new normal. . . . Why not redeploy this effort into a national citizen ID program that can be used for multiple purposes, including*

the secure delivery of government services, secure cross-border travel, and documentation of vaccination.[39]

"Digital wallet" suggests that economic activity could become an integral part of the frameworks' functions, a prospect that should terrify anyone but which Teyras describes as "really exciting." The UK's former Prime Minister and leading vaccine passport advocate Tony Blair also raised this possibility in an address to WEF members: "Digital ID can play a part in COVID but also if you think of the transactions that you want to do now with your customers, it's much simpler for them if they have a digital identity."[40]

Merging Your Health with Your Money

Many of the same companies and organizations that are driving the roll out of digital IDs are also pressing for the elimination of cash transactions. These companies and organizations include global banks, fintech start-ups, big tech giants, and credit card companies. The European Commission has already announced a plan to cap cash payments at €10,000 across the EU despite fierce opposition among cash-loving countries, such as Austria and Germany.

Of course, in a world of increasing government surveillance and control, cash is one of the last vestiges of personal freedom and privacy we have left.

"Cash gives people a sense of security, independence, and freedom," said Gernot Blümel, Austria's former finance minister. "We want to preserve that freedom for people."[41]

Other countries have other ideas, though. Even before the cash limit had been introduced, the French Government was advocating for a lower limit. Norbert Häring describes how this tactic conforms with IMF strategy to abolish cash even in the face of popular resistance: ". . . starting with a high, unoffensive limit and lowering it progressively."[42]

From the onset of the pandemic, cash has been suggested as a possible vector of infection. In early March 2020, in response to a question about whether banknotes could spread the coronavirus, a

World Health Organization (WHO) spokesperson said: "Yes, it's possible, and it's a good question. We know that money changes hands frequently and can pick up all sorts of bacteria and viruses . . . when possible it's a good idea to use contactless payments."[43]

Legacy media outlets pounced on the WHO's comments and magnified them, sparking fears over the safety of cash. The WHO has since walked back its comments, arguing that it was not advocating for people to abandon the use of cash, only that they should wash their hands after handling it.

Central banks have also attempted to dampen public fears. But at the same time many of those central banks, including the People's Bank of China, the Federal Reserve Bank, the European Central Bank, and the Bank of England, are exploring the possibility of introducing their own central bank digital currencies, or CBDCs, in the near future.

Combining digital currencies with digital IDs while phasing out, or even banning, the use of cash would grant governments and central banks the ability not only to track every purchase we make (and made in the past) but also to determine what we can and cannot spend our money on. They could also prevent certain "undesirable" people from buying anything. Anyone with a blocking notice attached to their digital identity would "thus be unable to do many of the most basic things independently," says Häring. Central banks could even issue stimulus funds with an expiration date, forcing people to spend rather than save.

Cash and CBDC are a world apart, as Agustín Carstens, the president of the Bank of International Settlements, the central bank of central banks, conceded in an interview:

> We don't know who's using a $100 bill today and we don't know who's using a 1,000 peso bill today. The key difference with the CBDC is the central bank will have absolute control on the rules and regulations that will determine the use of that expression of central bank liability, and also we will have the technology to enforce that.[44]

For central banks the introduction of CBDCs will provide a huge fillip to the power they already wield over the economy. It also means they will enter in direct competition with the banks they are supposed to regulate. Some economists have even warned that high street lenders, particularly smaller ones, could end up going under as savers switch their money into a secure digital account with their respective central bank at the slightest whiff of a financial crisis.

For the public, the benefits are less existent while the risks are huge. In the UK, a POLITICO survey of 2,500 adults found Brits "harbor more suspicion about central bank–backed digital currencies (CBDCs) than excitement." Just 24 percent of those surveyed believed the digital pound would bring more benefits than harm, while 30 percent said the opposite. Seventy-three percent of respondents expressed concern about the threat of cyberattacks and hackers. The prospect of losing payment privacy worried 70 percent.

Even proponents of CBDCs admit that central bank digital currency could have serious drawbacks, including further exacerbating income and wealth inequality.

"The rich might be more capable than others of taking advantage of new investment opportunities and reaping more of the benefits," says Eswar Prasad, a senior fellow at the Brookings Institute and author of *The Future of Money: How the Digital Revolution Is Transforming Currencies and Finance*. "As the economically marginalized have limited digital access and lack financial literacy, some of the changes could harm as much as they could help those segments of the population."[45]

So, not only will the introduction of CBDCs strip global citizens of one of the last vestiges of freedom, privacy, and anonymity (i.e., cash), it could also exacerbate the upward transfer of wealth that many societies have witnessed since the COVID-19 pandemic began. Together with the vaccine passports, CBDCs will facilitate even greater concentration of wealth and power—and not a moment too soon for the wealthy and powerful. As Häring argues in his forthcoming book *Endspiel des Kapitalismus* ("Endgame for Capitalism"), the elites are fully aware that the Ponzi scheme of late-stage capitalism, built upon the foundations of unpayable levels of public and private debt, will soon crash. Before that happens, they are trying to usher in a neofeudal society, in which they can continue to hold most of the power and wealth.

CHAPTER SEVEN

A Glimpse of the Future

IN 2014, THE CHINESE COMMUNIST PARTY unveiled a plan to create the world's first nationwide social credit system. It is, to put it mildly, one of the most comprehensive social control projects ever devised. The overarching goal is to track and monitor each and every Chinese citizen, business, and government agency in real time by amalgamating big data from public and private sources. That data is used to build a "high-trust society" in which individuals, companies, and organizations are strongly incentivized to follow the law and act ethically.

To that end, each individual, business, and government agency is allocated a social credit score based on their behavior. The State Council calls it a "credit system that covers the whole of society." When you follow the rules, obey Communist Party edicts, and behave like a "good citizen," you are awarded points. If you break the rules or otherwise act like a "bad citizen," you have points deducted. As *Foreign Policy* magazine reported in 2018, the ultimate goal for the Chinese government is to create a system that "allow[s] the trustworthy to roam everywhere under heaven while making it hard for the discredited to take a single step."[1]

The intent could not be clearer: Those ranked below a certain social credit score will form a literal underclass, forced to eke out a meager existence on the fringes of society. Sound familiar? Switch the word "trustworthy" for "vaccinated" and "discredited" for "unvaccinated," and the similarities are striking.

An Incomplete System

While the intent behind China's social credit system may be clear, the system's evolution on the ground is a lot less so. China is so big and the reach of its government so sprawling that keeping track of developments is extremely difficult. And of course, criticizing government policy in China can land a person in serious trouble. What's more, Western depictions of the system tend to be simplistic and overblown, as noted by *The Diplomat*, an international online news magazine covering geo-political trends and developments in the Indo-Pacific region, in 2019:

> *Criticism of the system, particularly from Western observers, has largely come along two, seemingly contradictory lines: that the project is either too ambitious to succeed or, given the country's successful clampdowns on dissent, too Orwellian to fail.*[2]

A case in point is a France 24 report from May 2019 claiming that "Chinese citizens' behavior is monitored and scrutinized—they are given scores and ranked according to rules set by the government." The reality is that this level of social control was—and still is—only happening in select parts of the country, in particular the cities where pilot social credit schemes are taking place.[3] And for the moment businesses are the main focus of attention. A MERICS study revealed that between 2003 and 2020, almost three quarters of mentions in official documents identified "companies" as the targets of social credit, compared to just 10 percent for individuals.[4]

The Chinese government wanted to have its social credit system up and running by the end of 2020, but that deadline has come and gone and the system is still far from complete. For the moment, it is still being piloted in approximately 30 cities around the country and the rollout across regions is extremely uneven. It is also still voluntary. The plan, set out in the "Planning Outline for the Construction of a Social Credit System (2014–2020)," is for it to eventually become mandatory and unified across the nation.[5]

The system is also heavily fragmented. Local governments chosen for the pilot schemes have developed their own social credit registers that coexist alongside private financial institutions' unofficial private social credit systems that award or deduct people points based on their online behavior. The most important of these systems are Tencent Credit, operated by WeChat, tech giant Tencent's messaging, social media, and mobile payment app, and Alipay's Sesame, or Zhima, Credit. Alipay is owned by Ant Group, which itself is an affiliate of the Chinese technology behemoth Ali Baba. Both Ali Baba and WeChat have hundreds of millions of monthly users.

According to a report by Chinese internet search company Sohu, users of Tencent Credit must input their real names and Chinese ID numbers to reveal their scores, which range from 300 to 850. WeChat split the score into five subcategories: consumption behavior, social connections, security, wealth, and compliance.[6]

Alipay's Sesame Credit system was first conceived by company executives in 2013 and launched two years later. As Mara Hvistendahl reported in her 2017 article for *Wired* magazine, "Inside China's Vast New Experiment in Social Ranking," the company's scope of influence is almost unfathomable:

> *If you live in the United States, you are by now accustomed to relinquishing your data to corporations. Credit card companies know when you run up bar tabs or buy sex toys. Facebook knows if you like Tasty cooking videos or Breitbart News. Uber knows where you go and how you behave en route. But Alipay knows all of these things about its users and more. Owned by Ant Financial, an affiliate of the massive Alibaba corporation, Alipay is sometimes called a super app. Its main competitor, WeChat, belongs to the social and gaming giant Tencent. Alipay and WeChat are less like individual apps than entire ecosystems.[7]*

Both Alipay and WeChat's social credit systems track shopping habits as well as other data to inform credit-style scores. These private systems operate on an opt-in basis, and though they tend to get conflated with the government plans, they aren't part of the official system. That said, the data collected by private companies is expected to be shared with the government in the future, and some of the data is already used in government trials. Sesame Credit says this occurs only with user consent.

We want people to be aware that their online behavior has an influence on their online credit score "so they know to behave themselves better," the WSJ quoted Joe Tsai, Alibaba's executive vice chairman, as saying.[8]

What's troubling is when these private systems are fused with the government rankings—which is already happening with some pilots. Mareike Ohlberg, research associate at the MERICS, told *Wired* magazine. "You'll have a sort of memorandum of understanding like arrangements between the city and, say, Alibaba and Tencent about data exchanges and including that in assessments of citizens."[9]

The Chinese government's social credit system has been marketed as a modified version of an individual's credit score. As Hvistendahl notes, over recent decades China grew at a breakneck speed to become the world's second largest economy, yet it never developed much of a functioning credit system:

> *The People's Bank of China, the country's central banking regulator, maintains records on millions of consumers, but they often contain little or no information. Until recently, it was difficult to get a credit card with any bank other than your own. Consumers mainly used cash. As housing prices spiked, this became increasingly untenable. "Now you need two suitcases to buy a house, not just one," says Zennon Kapron, who heads the financial tech consultancy Kapronasia. Still, efforts to establish a reliable credit system foundered because China lacked a third-party credit scoring entity.* [10]

That was what the government's social credit system was originally intended to be. In 2002, it was mentioned at the 16th Chinese Communist Party Congress as part of the Party's effort to create a "unified, open, competitive and orderly modern market system." The aim was to streamline the country's business environment, cut bureaucratic red tape, and create a means of keeping tabs on the creditworthiness and ethical standards of the millions of companies, domestic and foreign, operating in the country. In 2007, credit, tax, and contract performance records were suggested as potential elements of one's social credit status.

But as tends to happen with these sorts of projects, mission creep quickly set it. In 2014, Beijing published its so-called Planning

Outline for the Construction of a Social Credit System. The plan set out how the system would function as a nationwide incentive mechanism, by gathering social credit information from every individual, organization, and enterprise to reward good behavior and punish bad.

"A social credit system is an important component part of the Socialist market economy system and the social governance system," stated the document. "It is based on a complete network covering the credit records of members of society and credit infrastructure. It is supported by the lawful application of credit information and a credit services system."[11]

The ultimate goal is to "[raise] the honest mentality and credit levels of the entire society." To that end, all Chinese citizens would be rated in four main areas—administrative affairs, commercial activities, social behavior, and the law enforcement system. The core idea is that everyone gets a credit score and then earns or loses points depending on good or bad behavior. It's similar to a financial credit score but China's social credit system would broaden the concept to almost every facet of life.

"Good credit is turning into an asset," says Gang Zeng, the deputy director of the National Institute for Finance and Development, one of China's most influential think tanks. "For people with a good credit history, that asset will bring advantages, especially financially. If everybody cares about their good credit history it leads to an honest society."[12]

In some of the cities where the system is being piloted, such as Rongcheng in Shandong Province, each resident is given 1,000 points. Based on credit records and credit scores, evaluations are split into four categories: A, B, C, and D. If you accumulate 1,050 points, you are considered a triple-A model citizen (AAA). This confers benefits, such as access to lower interest on loans or discounts on travel. Between 1,030 and 1,049 points makes you a double-A citizen. If your score falls below 900, you're classed as a B.

A bad rating can make life a lot more difficult. Those qualified as a "C" (below 850) or a "D" (below 650) may struggle to book a business class seat on a plane, take out a loan, or send their child to a private school. Actions that can hurt one's credit rating include jaywalking, littering, speeding, falling behind on your debts, or cheating in exams or online games. Actions that can boost your credit rating include eating healthy food, athletic achievements, reporting other people for bad behavior, or donating bone marrow.[13]

So far, the localized social credit systems already in place have drawn little criticism from within China itself. One reason for this is that the system is still far from complete, meaning that many people are still not directly affected by it. Even in cities where the pilot schemes have taken place, participation is still voluntary. Many residents refuse to sign up because there are no meaningful benefits for doing so, says Dai Xin, an associate professor of legal theory at Peking University Law School.[14]

Many Chinese citizens also feel that the social credit system's ostensible end—encouraging more trustworthy social behavior by individuals and businesses—justifies the means. There is, after all, a significant trust deficit in many areas of Chinese business and society. In 2018, a 32-year-old entrepreneur, who gave his name only as Chen, told *Foreign Policy* magazine he felt that "people's behaviour ha[d] gotten better and better" since the launch of the pilot scheme. "For example, when we drive now, we always stop in front of crosswalks. If you don't stop, you will lose your points. At first, we just worried about losing points, but now we are accustomed to it."[15]

A 2019 study by Genia Kostka, a professor of Chinese politics at the Freie Universität Berlin, published by *SAGE Journals* suggests that the extent to which Chinese citizens' approve of the social credit systems may depend on their social position and status:

> *Based on a cross-regional survey, the study finds a surprisingly high degree of approval of SCSs across respondent groups. Interestingly, more socially advantaged citizens (wealthier, better-educated, and urban residents) show the strongest approval of SCSs, along with older people. While one might expect such knowledgeable citizens to be most concerned about the privacy implications of SCS, they instead appear to embrace SCSs because they interpret it through frames of benefit-generation and promoting honest dealings in society and the economy instead of privacy-violation.*[16]

The seeming broad public acceptance of social credit schemes in China might also reflect the severity of punishment that can follow speaking out against the government. There is also a cultural dimension at work. The Chinese have a very different notion of privacy from their Western counterparts. In traditional Confucian philosophy, morality trumps respect for individual rights as the guiding principle for interpersonal relationships and the government of a society, notes Eunsun Cho in her paper, "The Social Credit System: Not Just Another Chinese Idiosyncrasy," published in Princeton's *Journal for International and Public Affairs*. It also helps that Chinese people are already accustomed to surveillance:

> *Since the Mao era, the Chinese government has kept* dang'an, *a secret dossier, on millions of its urban residents that maintains influence in the public sector to this day (Jacobs 2015; Yang 2011). The information included in the dossier ranges from one's educational and work performance, family background, and records of self-criticism to mental health conditions, but individuals do not have access to their* dang'an *(Ibid.). When a completely opaque system like* dang'an *has been in place for decades, an intrusive program like the SCS may feel less objectionable to the Chinese public.*
>
> *Big data surveillance is already in place across the country. In Xinjiang, an autonomous region in western China home to Uighur Muslim minority, the government is collecting a vast array of citizens' information—including but not limited to DNA samples, iris scans, voice samples, applications installed on phones, and records of power consumption—in order to search for "suspected criminals."[17]*

Additional Tools of Repression

The term "social credit system" is a misnomer, says the Asan Institute for Policy Studies, a South Korean nonprofit think tank: "This has nothing to do with credit; it has everything to do with control. Marrying algorithms to big data, the Chinese government seeks to inculcate a higher standard of morality and tighten its control over the people."[18]

But the system is "incredibly messy," according to Vincent Brussee, an associate analyst at MERICS. There are literally thousands of government documents that mention credit or social credit. Instead of functioning as one giant centralized system, as Western media often portray it, China's social credit system is "more of a loose-hanging policy framework for social credit systems," says Brusee. For example, different cities, ministries, and departments all have their own interpretation of what it means to be trustworthy or untrustworthy.[19]

But the system is only one part of China's huge surveillance and enforcement apparatus. There are also the blacklists that predate the social credit system, which the government uses to block financial transgressors from accessing basic services, such as public transport. The lists are publicly searchable on a government website called *Credit China.*

In April 2018, the government-affiliated news website *Global Times* reported that more than 11 million flights and 4.25 million high-speed train trips had been blocked for so-called "discredited people."[20] A year later, *Forbes* reported that as many as 23 million people had been banned from travel. Grounds for inclusion on Beijing's no-fly or no-train lists include failure to pay fines on time or taxes when told to as well as engaging in financial fraud or false advertising.[21]

Talking about the wrong sorts of things can also land you in trouble. Liu Hu, a journalist in China who covers censorship and government corruption, found himself on a List of Dishonest Persons Subject to Enforcement by the Supreme People's Court. As a result, he was disqualified from buying a plane ticket and banned from traveling some train lines, buying property, or taking out a loan.

"There was no file, no police warrant, no official advance notification. They just cut me off from the things I was once entitled to," Liu Hu told *The Globe and Mail.* "What's really scary is there's nothing you can do about it. You can report to no one. You are stuck in the middle of nowhere."[22]

Local governments also use public shaming to punish transgressors. In its trial of the social credit system the local government of Suzhou, Anhui province, went so far as to publish on its WeChat account photos of local residents walking around the city in their pajamas. The officials said the people were made an example of as part of a drive to "expose uncivilized behaviors and improve citizens' quality." The images posted on WeChat were caught by surveillance cameras and included private data, such as the person's name and ID card number.[23]

This points to another key instrument of social control in China: the government's vast, AI-powered surveillance system. China has more surveillance cameras per person than any other country on the planet—no small feat for a country of 1.44 billion people. Of the 770 million surveillance cameras in use globally in 2018, 54 percent of them were in China, according to IHS Markit's 2019 report on the sector. China is also home to 16 of the top 20 most surveilled cities on the planet (based on the number of cameras per 1,000 people), says consumer website *Comparitech*. London, by the way, is the third most surveilled city on the planet.[24]

China also boasts the world's biggest manufacturer of surveillance cameras, Hikvision, whose facilities can crank out 260,000 cameras per day. According to a 2021 article in *The Atlantic* called "China Is Watching You," that's the equivalent of "two for every three people born each day." In 2019, the company manufactured almost a quarter of the world's surveillance cameras.[25]

The Leading Edge of a Global Trend

China may be leading the way when it comes to keeping digital tabs on its citizens as well as manufacturing the tools to do so, but it is by no means an outlier. By the end of 2021, it is estimated that over one billion surveillance cameras will have been installed in the world.[26] With the exception of Taiyuan and Wuxi, both in China, London is home to more surveillance cameras per capita than any other city on the planet.[27] According to IHS, the United States had almost as many surveillance and security cameras as China in 2018, with one for roughly every 4.6 people (compared to China's 1 for every 4.1). The UK was not far behind with one for every 6.5.

"During the past few years, coverage of the surveillance market has focused heavily on China's massive deployments of cameras and artificial intelligence (AI) technology," said IHS Markit analyst Oliver Philippou. "What's received far less attention is the high level of penetration of surveillance cameras in the United States. With the United States nearly on par with China in terms of camera penetration, future debate over mass surveillance is likely to concern America as much as China."[28]

The United Kingdom and the United States are also investing heavily in facial recognition technologies. Both countries have been trialing live facial recognition (LFR) surveillance in public places for a number of years. Police and security forces in the two countries are also making use of retrospective facial recognition (RFR), which is even more controversial than LFR. While LFR compares live images with those on a specific watch list, RFR enables police to check against a far broader collection of sources, including CCTV feeds and social media.

"Those deploying it can in effect turn back the clock to see who you are, where you've been, what you have done and with whom, over many months or even years," Ella Jakubowska, policy advisor at European Digital Rights, an advocacy group, told *Wired* magazine, adding that the technology can "suppress people's free expression, assembly and ability to live without fear."[29]

In the European Union a tug of war has broken out between privacy advocates and security forces over proposed legislation for the use of remote biometric identification, such as facial recognition, in public. Proponents of the technology, including law enforcement agencies, argue that it is needed to catch criminals. But privacy activists and some European lawmakers have called for an outright ban. They include Wojciech Wiewiórowski, who leads the EU's in-house data protection authority, EDPS, which is supposed to ensure the EU's own agencies are complying with the Continent's strict privacy rules.

Wiewiórowski warns that use of the technology would "turn society, turn our citizens, turn the places we live, into places where we are permanently recognizable. I'm not sure if we are really as a society ready for that."[30]

In early December, the civil liberties group Statewatch reported that the Council of the EU, where the senior ministers of the 27 Member States sit, not only intends to extend the purposes for which biometric systems can be used under the EU's proposed Artificial Intelligence Act but is also seeking to allow private actors to operate mass biometric surveillance systems on behalf of police forces.[31]

Moves like this, which accelerate the drift of ostensibly democratic societies and nations toward technocratic authoritarianism, are often presented by the political, business, and financial elite as unavoidable. The technology already exists and is broadly beneficial, at least to those in power, while also opening up yet another rich vein of opportunities for tech giants, so why not use it?

A perfect example of this way of thinking is the book *The Age of AI: And Our Human Future*, written by Henry Kissinger, for whom no introduction is needed; Eric Schmidt, the former CEO of Google who has forged close ties to the United States' military and security industrial complexes; and Daniel Huttenlocher, the dean of MIT's Schwarzman College of Computing, an AI-focused mega-lab that is partly funded by foreclosure profiteer Stephen Schwarzman, the cofounder of the investment group Blackstone. As Meredith Whittaker and Lucy Suchman note in their article, "The Myth of Artificial Intelligence," published in *The American Prospect*, the book serves "Big Tech's agenda through three rhetorical strategies":

> *First, they position Big Tech's AI and computing power as critical national infrastructure, across research and development environments, and military and government operations. Second, they propose "solutions" that serve to vastly enrich tech companies, helping them to meet their profit and growth projections, while also funding AI-focused research programs at top-tier universities. This serves to bring Big Tech and academia closer together, further merging their interests and deterring meaningful dissent by a new wave of researchers critical of Silicon Valley. Third, and most importantly, by providing arguments against curbing the power of*

Big Tech companies, the book frames these companies as too import-ant to the American national interest to regulate or to break up. [32]

Western governments are also beginning to embrace social credit systems, albeit on a small scale—for now—and by instituting reward schemes rather than punitive measures. In October, the UK government announced it was launching a pilot scheme called HeadUp to encourage people to wear wrist-worn devices that can generate personalized health recommendations, such as increasing their step count, eating more fruits and vegetables, and decreasing portion size. The government says that "healthy behaviours . . . will unlock rewards, which could include gym passes, clothes or food vouchers and discounts for shops, cinema or theme park tickets":

Evidence suggests that financial incentives can improve rates of physical activity and inspire healthier eating so HeadUp will work with a range of organisations to provide rewards such as vouchers, merchandise, discounts and gift cards.

The government is committed to helping people lead healthier, happier lives by making it easier for people to make healthy choices. [33]

A similar app was launched in Canada back in 2016, called Carrot Rewards, which awarded users points in return for completing questionnaires and following steps for healthy living. The app was rolled out in in three Canadian provinces (British Colombia, Newfoundland, and Labrador) and one territory (Northwest Territories) before the app designer ran out of funds in 2019. But that was not the end of the Carrot Rewards system. In January 2020, the London-based health app-developer Optimity bought Carrot Rewards and relaunched the health app under a new model.[34]

The Carrot Rewards system reveals an interesting feature of the social credit systems being developed and rolled out in both the West and China: Most of them are run by private businesses, not government. While these sorts of systems are pretty harmless on their own, at least in their current form, it is ironic that governments such as the UK are considering making healthy eating part of a social credit–based scheme while public health officials in the country—as well as many others—have systematically ignored the role healthy eating, exercising, taking supplements, and other preventive measures could play in reducing the risk of COVID-19.

In 2019, the business magazine *Fast Company* ran an article titled "Uh Oh: Silicon Valley Is Building a Chinese-style Social Credit System." In it, journalist Mike Elgan explained how a change in US law had allowed life insurance companies to use the sort of behavior displayed in their customers' social media posts to inform the premiums they charge them. "The insurance companies have to demonstrate that social media evidence points to risk, and not be based on discrimination of any kind—they can't use social posts to alter premiums based on race or disability, for example."

In this context, it is interesting that Airbnb can ban customers for life for any reason it chooses, and without the right of appeal. A message on the company's website notes it is not obligated to divulge why action is taken against an account. Airbnb has awarded itself broad latitude to ban users indefinitely if they have convictions the company deems "serious" without explaining what it means by "serious." In September 2020 a coalition of activist groups including ACLU sent a letter to the San Francisco–based company complaining that its use of arrest and conviction records to screen prospective users perpetuates the racism prevalent in the criminal legal system and demanding that the company reverse course.

"As many as 100 million adults in the United States—or nearly a third of the total population—have a conviction record of some sort," said Marlon Peterson, Atlantic Fellow for Racial Equity. "I know from personal experience that while many of these convictions occurred years ago, Airbnb has decided to perpetually punish those with a conviction record long after they have paid their debt to society."[35]

Uber has a similar policy allowing it to ban drivers from using the service if their rating falls significantly below average. Messaging apps like Whatsapp are also banning or terminating users if they send spam or threatening messages or if they have been blocked by other users. In October 2021 the company, owned by Facebook (now called Meta), banned two million users in India alone.[36]

As Elgan warns, the most disturbing attribute of any social credit system, whether run by a government or a private-sector company, is not its invasiveness but the fact that it's extralegal:

> *Crimes are punished outside the legal system, which means no presumption of innocence, no legal representation, no judge, no jury, and often no appeal. In other words, it's an alternative legal system where the accused have fewer rights.*
>
> *Social credit systems are an end-run around the pesky complications of the legal system. Unlike China's government policy, the social credit system emerging in the US is enforced by private companies. If the public objects to how these laws are enforced, it can't elect new rule-makers.*
>
> *An increasing number of societal "privileges" related to transportation, accommodations, communications, and the rates we pay for services (like insurance) are either controlled by technology companies or affected by how we use technology services. And Silicon Valley's rules for being allowed to use their services are getting stricter.*
>
> *If current trends hold, it's possible that in the future a majority of misdemeanors and even some felonies will be punished not by Washington, D.C., but by Silicon Valley. It's a slippery slope away from democracy and toward corporatocracy.*
>
> *In other words, in the future, law enforcement may be determined less by the Constitution and legal code, and more by end-user license agreements.* [37]

Wall Street banks could soon be getting in on the act as well. In 2020, the International Monetary Fund (IMF) featured research on its website suggesting that lenders are considering using data from borrowers' internet browsing, search, and shopping history to create a more accurate credit score:

> *The use of non-financial data will have large effects on the provision of financial services. Traditionally, banks rely on the*

analysis of customer financial information from payment flows and accounting records. The rise of the internet permits the use of new types of non-financial customer data, such as browsing histories and online shopping behavior of individuals, or customer ratings for online vendors.

The literature suggests that such non-financial data are valuable for financial decision making. Berg et al. (2019) show that easy-to-collect information such as the so-called "digital footprint" (email provider, mobile carrier, operating system, etc.) performs as well as traditional credit scores in assessing borrower risk. Moreover, there are complementarities between financial and non-financial data: combining credit scores and digital footprint further improves loan default predictions. Accordingly, the incorporation of non-financial data can lead to significant efficiency gains in financial intermediation.[38]

In other words, our internet habits could soon have a bearing on whether or not banks will lend to us, how much they will be willing to lend and at what interest rate.

We have also seen how Silicon Valley giants like Facebook and Twitter have become the arbitrators of truth in recent years, largely at the insistence of government. This has led to a bizarre situation in which fact-checkers, programmers, and AI algorithms remove content provided by scientific experts in fields such as virology, epidemiology, medicine, or pharmacology if the content in question does not chime with the prevailing official narrative.

In December 2021, the disinformation war took an even darker turn when Twitter quietly updated its "COVID-19 misleading information policy" to impose new sanctions on tweets claiming, among other things, that people who are fully vaccinated can "spread or shed the virus" to others. This means Twitter users could now be sanctioned for sharing or discussing a scientific fact that has been proven by countless studies and is even admitted by the Centers for Disease Control and Prevention (CDC). The change in policy produced a fierce backlash from users and on December 14, Twitter announced its use of the word "virus" had been no more than a typo. What it had apparently intended to say was that it would sanction claims that the fully vaccinated can (emphasis my own) "spread or shed the *vaccine*" to others.[39]

We have already seen social media companies, such as Twitter and Facebook, ban users for creating or sharing the "wrong" sort of content. If this practice begins to proliferate as much as it has in India and users' social media activity becomes tied to a digital ID or social credit score, posting or sharing contentious information on a controversial topic, such as, say, vaccines, might not only lead to censorship and banning, but could also have a negative impact on a person's social status and their ability to access certain services. In other words, we can bid farewell to free speech.

Beyond All Recognition

Since Elgan's article was published in August 2019, the situation has deteriorated beyond all recognition. COVID-19 arrived in early 2020 and has not departed, despite the rollout of the vaccines. Many of the world's so-called liberal democracies have taken advantage of the crisis it has triggered to bulldoze into law batteries of repressive measures, many of them enabled by digital technologies. Those technologies, including vaccine passports and other forms of digital identity, have provided states with unprecedented mass surveillance and control powers.

Few countries have traveled quite so far down this road as Australia, which has imposed one of the longest lockdowns on the planet. It is also forcibly confining individuals—many of them perfectly healthy—to "quarantine camps." In December 2021, the state of Victoria, home to Australia's second largest city, Melbourne, passed new pandemic laws that grant the state's premier, Daniel Andrews, the power to declare a pandemic for an unlimited period of time. The new bill, designed to replace sweeping state of emergency powers, also gives the health minister the authority to issue "any order" he deems necessary, including lockdowns and vaccine mandates.

Victorian Bar President Christopher Blanden QC described the proposed laws as "extreme," adding for emphasis that the Stasi, the secret police in communist East Germany, would be more than happy with such a "breathtaking" range of powers. Blanden also said the bill did not contain sufficient checks and balances, gave the premier too much power with scant parliamentary scrutiny, and allowed for indefinite detention of people who breach the restrictions.[40]

In England and Wales, a new police bill is awaiting passage (as of this writing) that will effectively enshrine lockdown-like restrictions on the right to protest. The new bill contains myriad restrictions on demonstrations as well as new surveillance and stop-and-search powers, notes Jun Pang, policy and campaigns officer at Liberty, a UK-based human rights advocacy group:

> *The right through which we won many of the things we take for granted today—from voting rights to marriage equality—which allows all of us to stand up against injustice. Now we know the government is taking a sledgehammer to this right, smashing everyone's ability to stand up to power . . .*
>
> *[The new bill will also create] new Serious Disruption Prevention Orders, or protest-banning orders, which can be imposed on people if they have previously been convicted of what the amendment calls a 'protest-related offence'—or even if they have just been to two protests in the past five years in which they carried out activities that could have caused serious disruption. The government just this week proposed an expansive, catch-all definition of serious disruption, which can also be redefined in the future by the home secretary of the day.*
>
> *Protest-banning orders can require people to keep police up to date on their current residence and can include restrictions on who people can meet, where they go and when, and their use of the internet. Breach of these conditions could lead to a 51-week jail sentence, an unlimited fine or both.*[41]

In the United States multiple cities, from New York to Los Angeles, have rolled out vaccine passports. In November, the House of

Representatives passed a bill, with the support of 80 Republicans, to set up a federal vaccination database. If the Senate also passes the bill, the federal government will spend $400 million on an "immunization system data modernization and expansion," a system it describes as "a confidential, population-based, computerized database that records immunization doses administered by any health care provider to persons within the geographic area covered by that database."[42] This could end up being the tracking system to which a digital vaccine passport is tied.

But it is Europe that is truly leading the way, where almost all nations have embraced unprecedented tech-enabled control and segregation of society.

Even the Chinese Communist Party must be impressed. Since the early days of the pandemic, Beijing has been calling for a global COVID-19 tracking system using QR codes, to help reopen international travel and business. Speaking at the virtual G20 last year President Xi said that countries needed to coordinate a uniform set of policies and standards to ensure the "smooth functioning" of the world economy during and post pandemic:

> *China has proposed a global mechanism on the mutual recognition of health certificates based on nucleic acid test results in the form of internationally accepted QR codes. We hope more countries will join this mechanism.* [43]

Like the Chinese with the social credit system, most Europeans have so far accepted the imposition of vaccine passports. According to a survey by the British polling company YouGov (which, it is worth noting, was cofounded and is still partly owned by the UK's former vaccine minister, Nadhim Zahawi), a majority of people in the UK (64 percent), Spain (64 percent), Italy (62 percent), Sweden (62 percent), Germany (59 percent), and France (57 percent) support the use of vaccine passports for large public events. Fifty-eight percent of Italians, 54 percent of Germans, 51 percent of Spaniards and 50 percent of French people support using them to control access to restaurants.[44]

The Power of Fear

None of this should come as much of a surprise. When people are sufficiently frightened and confused, they can be easily controlled. As British writer Paul Kingsnorth notes in "How Fear Fuels the Vaccine Wars," of all the stories we are watching play out right now, this is the biggest one: "the manipulation of public fear to impose unprecedented levels of control on populations":

> *The ongoing nature of the COVID threat—the endless boosters, the endless variants—means there is no end in sight to this "new normal." Like the War on Terror before it, the control and monitoring of citizens in the name of "public health," the segregation of the virtuous vaxxed (or, any day now, boosted) from the anti- social unvaxxed, the internet-wide censorship of whatever Silicon Valley labels "disinformation," and the widespread obedience of the once-mainstream press to an agreed story towards which they clum- sily try to nudge their readers—none of this has any sell-by date.*[45]

That the vaccine passports are issued for vaccines that do not confer immunity or prevent transmission does not seem to matter. By late November 2021—five months after Brussels's introduction of the Green Pass—Europe was once again the epicenter of global COVID-19 infections. By the end of the year many of the countries in Europe with the highest caseloads on a per capita basis, such as Ireland, Gibraltar, Italy, Spain, Portugal, and Iceland, also had the highest vaccination rates. Indeed, since Rome banned unvaccinated Italians from working, cases have done nothing but rise. In France, one of the first countries to ban people without vaccine passports from accessing hospitality venues, case numbers began rising expo- nentially in mid-October and by January 2022 were almost four times higher than at the previous peak, in November 2020.

All of these trends represent a damning indictment of a deeply flawed policy. Indeed, it could even be argued that the launch of the Green Pass, and all the national iterations it has spawned, has led to more coronavirus infections, not fewer. According to Belgian micro- biologist Emmanuel André, when Belgium's COVID Safe Ticket

(CST) was introduced, not only did it lead to a negligible increase in vaccine uptake, but public events that required a CST were allowed to drop the face mask and social distancing measures:

> *Therefore, the CST led to the opposite of what was expected, also because other measures were phased out when it was introduced . . . Masks, alongside the vaccine and good ventilation, remain one of the most important ways of protecting against the virus.* [46]

In any sane, rational world, the failure of Europe's Green Pass system to contain the virus would have been enough to force a dramatic policy rethink. But instead, the continent's policymakers have doubled down on their failed strategy. When Austria began registering more daily COVID cases than at any time since the pandemic, the government responded by imposing the world's first ever "lockdown of the unvaccinated." It lasted for five days before the government extended the lockdown to everybody. But the precedent had been set. Two weeks later, Germany followed suit, banning unvaccinated people from all but the most essential businesses.

Austria has even unveiled plans to mandate vaccines for every resident in the country over the age of 14, becoming the first so-called democratic nation to take such a step. Under the proposed bill, anyone above that age (including teenagers) who refuses to get the COVID-19 jab after February 2022, when vaccination becomes mandatory, will face a fine of up to €3,600.[47] Germany is considering a similar measure.[48] In Greece, which already has some of the highest poverty rates in Europe, authorities will start fining people over the age of 60 who are not vaccinated €100 for every month they remain unvaccinated after January 15.

Zero Transparency

Most ominous of all, European Commission President Ursula von der Leyen has called for a debate on EU-wide mandatory vaccination. The proposal is plagued with problems, not least of which is the fact that the vaccine does not prevent transmission or infection, or that vaccine manufacturers are exempt from liability.[49] But there's an even more contentious issue: the lack of transparency around the agreements between the European Commission and vaccine manufacturers. Five Members of the European Parliment (MEPs) from the Greens/EFA Group have even submitted a case application to the European Court of Justice alleging "implicit refusal" from the Commission to provide access to information regarding the vaccine contracts.

"For nine months the Commission has refused to disclose them, but after being heavily criticised for the opacity of its vaccine policy, they have published heavily redacted contracts," which is "clearly insufficient," said Kim van Sparrentak, a Dutch MEP.[50]

In April, the *New York Times* reported that von der Leyen had exchanged calls and texts with Pfizer CEO Albert Bourla. (It is also worth noting that as of December 2020 von der Leyen's husband, Heiko von der Leyen, has been working as Medical Director of the US biotech company Orgenesis, which specializes in cell and gene therapies, including vaccines.[51]) Yet when MEPs requested to access the content of von der Leyen's messages with Bourla, the Commission said it had no record of them. Text messages, the Commission contends, are generally "short-lived" and in principle excluded from its record-keeping.

The Commission refuses to confirm whether the correspondence has been deleted, whether they still exist, or whether the Commission just doesn't know. This is not the first time that von der Leyen has found herself in trouble over deleted text messages, reports *Der Spiegel*:

> *In late 2019, it emerged that text messages had been deleted from two of the official mobile phones she used during her time as Germany's defense minister, leading to a criminal complaint against von der Leyen and trouble with an investigative committee in the German parliament that had requested the text messages as evidence.*[52]

So, to recap, the European Commission president has called for a debate on making COVID-19 vaccination mandatory across

Europe despite the fact the vaccines do little to prevent transmission or infection of COVID-19. Additionally, most European lawmakers have no access to the contracts the Commission signed with vaccine makers in March 2021. The Commission president herself, who may have conflicts of interest, appears to have destroyed communications she has had with the CEO of the world's biggest vaccine manufacturer. All while the EU leads the way in forcing digital IDs onto its almost 450 million citizens.

Romanian MEP Cristian Terheş describes it like this:

> Clearly what we are witnessing right now is the Chinafication of Europe. What is happening in China with social credit scores . . . we are seeing the same . . . being implemented right now . . . in the European Union. The Green Certificate was just the first step. There are more proposals under debate in the parliament. The European Wallet ID, the European Social Security Card—all these things that are creating a system that will monitor, control, supervise, and condition the rights of all European citizens.[53]

But even in Europe, not everyone is on board, despite the increasingly authoritarian measures being implemented by both the European Commission and national governments. As von der Leyen herself admitted, roughly one third of all Europeans, including most children under the age of eleven, were still unvaccinated as of late November. This is despite the huge pressure governments are exerting on citizens to toe the line.

And as I will show in chapter 8, despite monumental efforts to parlay the COVID-19 pandemic to cement power and control over the world's citizens, resistance is rising around the world.

CHAPTER EIGHT

The Resistance Is Now (or Never)

As 2021 DREW TO A CLOSE, the world seemed to be in an even darker place than it was a year prior. In the largest live medical experiment ever conducted, "miracle" vaccines were rolled out across the planet—at least, to those who can afford them—and injected into the arms of billions of people. By the end of 2021, it had become clear they are not nearly as effective or as safe as we'd been led to believe. There are now far more daily cases of COVID-19 than at any other time in the pandemic.

Even the most ardent supporters of the new, non-sterilizing vaccine technologies admit that the vaccines do not prevent transmission of the virus. They are incredibly leaky against the Delta variant and even more so against Omicron. "Especially with Omicron, where we don't see virtually any difference, there is a very narrow gap between people vaccinated and non-vaccinated, both can get infected with a virus, more or less at the same pace," said Professor Cyrille Cohen, head of Immunology at Bar-Ilan University and a member of the advisory committee for vaccines for the Israeli Government.[1]

In Denmark, the public health authorities, which have generally done a good job of tracking COVID-19 case numbers as well as the emergence and spread of new variants, reported in late December 2021 that 89.7 percent of the 17,800 Danes who had contracted Omicron by December 15 had been vaccinated two or three times. Only 8.5 percent were unvaccinated. By contrast, the unvaccinated accounted for 23.7 percent of the people who had contracted Delta or other variants. This is in a country where just under 80 percent of the population had received two vaccines and 35 percent had received a booster. It is a similar story in the UK where cases per 100,000 were higher in the vaccinated than in the unvaccinated, according to the government's vaccine report of January 13, 2022.

These findings suggest that Omicron is not only completely evading the vaccines but may even infect the vaccinated more than the unvaccinated. Put simply, this is a vaccine that is falling part. On January 11, 2022, the World Health Organization (WHO) warned that Omicron represented "a new west-to-east tidal wave" that could end up infecting more than half of the population living in Europe—the world's most vaccinated continent—within the next two months. In Europe, some governments were calling for the COVID-19 virus to be reclassified as endemic, meaning that it is here to stay but is no longer considered a public health emergency. One of the reasons for this is that public health agencies have essentially lost control of the virus' spread. In my country of residence, Spain, cases had soared so high that the country's diagnostic labs could not keep up with the demand for tests, as *El País* reported on January 17.[2]

The only silver lining on offer was that Omicron appeared to be less virulent than other dominant variants. At the time of writing this, it is too early to tell with total confidence just how true that is. We probably won't know until the virus begins infecting large numbers of elderly patients in countries with old populations. If Omicron does turn out to be a lot milder than previous dominant variants, then perhaps, just perhaps, it means we are beginning to finally turn the corner of this global health crisis. But we should still be wary. Given its extreme contagiousness, Omicron still has the potential to overwhelm our heavily weakened hospital and primary care systems. Omicron also appears to be generating more symptomatic cases among young children, which is a major cause for concern. And while it doesn't target the respiratory system like previous variants, there are unsettling signs that it may be hitting other organs proportionally harder than other variants. There are also likely to be more variants in the pipeline, one or more of which could end up being more virulent than Omicron.

Yet even as more and more governments call for a reduction of quarantine times, which is almost certain to increase the risk of contagion, the end of testing and a loosening of mask mandates, they continue to double down on the vaccine mandates and ratchet up the vaccine passport requirements. Almost every country in Europe, Australasia, and North America, from France to Germany, to Australia and New Zealand, to Canada and Belgium, to Spain and Italy, called an abrupt end to decades—or in some cases, centuries—of liberal democracy. In its place they have adopted a new form of governance in which basic rights are trampled in the name of bringing a virus under control, with a substandard medical therapy that delivers no such promise.

Building a Global Biosecurity State

The ultimate goal, it seems, is to set up a global biosecurity state. On December 1, the WHO announced plans to kickstart a process "to draft and negotiate a convention, agreement or other international instrument under the Constitution of the World Health Organization to strengthen pandemic prevention, preparedness, and response."[3] Once again, the European Union appears to be playing a key role in pushing for this "global pandemic treaty."[4]

Given how badly most governments have responded to the COVID-19 pandemic and how poorly states have coordinated their containment efforts, there is an argument to be made for establishing pandemic control processes and standards at a global level. However, a centralized global pandemic response under the auspices of an organization like the WHO will mean that health authorities will be even less answerable to local populations. One thing that is clear is that the WHO, in its current form, is not the body to do it.

The organization has already done a shoddy enough job of combatting the current pandemic. For example, it failed to recognize that the COVID-19 virus was an airborne disease until far too late. It also fought, at every step, to discourage national health authorities from using cheap, off-patent medicines such as ivermectin in the early treatment of COVID-19 patients. Both of these failings have cost an untold number of lives. The WHO is also heavily conflicted by the donations it receives from private companies, many in the pharmaceutical industry, and private trusts, such as the Gates and Rockefeller foundations, both at the forefront of efforts to push global digital identity on the world's population. Those donations now account for 80 percent of the organization's funding. [5]

In other words, if the WHO took full control of all future responses to global pandemics, it would represent yet another corporate takeover of government functions—this time at a global level. Additionally, the World Economic Forum now holds a huge amount of sway over the United Nations following a strategic partnership agreement in 2019 (see chapter 6). Unless stopped in its tracks, the construction of a global biosecurity state could pave the way to a neo-feudal system of global government whereby a tiny fraction of the global population owns and controls everything and global corporations call the shots. The rest of us will own nothing, have no privacy, no control over our own bodies, and have little choice but to do what we are told because our every action will be connected to our digital identity.

Even before COVID, we were already quite far along this path. For decades Wall Street and the City of London had made an artform of "extract[ing] rents through market-based forms of daylight robbery", as the economist and former Greek Finance Minister Yanis Varoufakis pointed out in a 2020 article, "Techno Feudalism Is Taking Over." Since the financial crisis of 2008, two further developments have intensified this shift: First, the global economy began to be "powered by the constant generation of central bank money, not by private profit," says Varoufakis. At the same time, value extraction "increasingly shifted away from markets and onto digital platforms, like Facebook and Amazon, which no longer operate like oligopolistic firms, but rather like private fiefdoms or estates."[6]

The recent creation of biosecurity states across the former liberal West promises to turbocharge this shift toward tech-enabled neo-feudalism. In most countries in Europe, you now need to take a COVID-19 vaccine every few months to be allowed to do even the most basic of things, from going to work to eating in a restaurant, to shopping in the local mall, to even seeing your general practitioner. In Germany and Austria, the unvaccinated are under virtual house arrest. In Italy, they can't work or attend baptisms, communions, and weddings. They can't even ride the bus or metro and everyone over 50 now faces mandatory vaccination. In many countries, anyone who refuses the booster shot, even after suffering a severe adverse reaction from a prior shot, is fated to join the burgeoning ranks of the unvaccinated, the new global class of untouchables.

Many of the world's wealthiest have massively expanded their wealth and power in the last two years, largely on the back of central bank money printing. As Varoufakis says, "all over the West, central banks print money that financiers lend to corporations, which then use it to buy back their shares (whose prices have decoupled from profits)." The closer you are to the money spigot, the easier it is to expand your wealth. All the while, small, independent businesses that were functioning perfectly well before the pandemic but were forced to take on debt just to weather last year's lockdowns are collapsing as economic conditions deteriorate.

Many of the world's poorest are finding it hard even to feed themselves, thanks in part to surging food inflation. In Latin America and the Caribbean, the region hardest hit by the pandemic, the number of people facing extreme hunger rose by 13.8 million in 2020 alone, to 60 million people. That's roughly 10 percent of the region's population. A staggering 267 million people—almost half the population—grappled with food insecurity in 2020.[7] Something people in advanced economies tend to forget or simply are not aware of is that every time a lockdown occurs in the Global North, struggling economies in the Global South feel the effects even more keenly, as demand for their raw materials, assembled goods or tourism destinations collapses.

We cannot say we were not warned. As the Germany-based playwright, author, and satirist C. J. Hopkins notes, the global political, financial, and business elite telegraphed all of this to us during the first lockdowns of March 2020; most of us were just too disoriented and shell-shocked to listen:

> *They informed us in unmistakable terms that our lives were about to change, forever. They branded and advertised this change as "the New Normal," in case we were . . . you know, cognitively*

challenged. They did not hide it. They wanted us to understand exactly what was coming, a global-capitalist version of totalitarianism, in which we will all be happy little fascist "consumers" showing each other our "compliance certificates" in order to be allowed to live our lives. [8]

But there is still cause for optimism. All around the world, pockets of resistance are forming at the same time that overall public faith in the COVID-19 vaccines appears to be falling. As governments slide further and further into authoritarianism, demanding ever more stringent compliance from their respective populations, that resistance is growing. And it is taking many forms, from legal challenges in the courts, to campaigns to encourage the use of cash, to consumer boycotts, to huge—and growing—popular demonstrations in towns and cities all over the world. More and more people, it seems, are waking from their slumber.

Legal Fightback

On November 30, 2021, Namur's Court of First Instance, in the Wallonia region of Belgium, ruled that the country's vaccine passport—the so-called "COVID Safe Ticket" (CST)—was illegal. According to the ruling, government legislation requiring all citizens to show their CST before entering cafés, restaurants, gyms, and cultural venues represented a disproportionate curb on individual freedoms that does not even serve the goal they are ostensibly intended for: to control the transmission of COVID-19.

The court also warned that the CST may contravene European law as well as the right to the protection of personal data. The judges ruled that the region "must take all the measures it deems appropriate to put an end to this situation of apparent inequality resulting from the use of CST in the Walloon region."[9] If the Walloon Government didn't do so within seven days of the judgement, it would be subject to a fine of €5,000 for every day it continues to enforce the use of the CST.

Wallonia's regional government announced it would appeal the decision. And on January 7, 2022, the Liège court of appeal ruled in its favor, declaring that while the CST does indeed infringe on the freedoms of every Belgian, it is a "necessary, objective and proportional" instrument needed to contain the COVID-19 epidemic.[10]

The case was brought by a nonprofit organization called Notre Bon Droit ("Our Good Right"), which describes itself as an "alliance of health professionals, scientists, lawyers and Belgian citizens who believe that the government's response to COVID-19 is misguided and not based on the best scientific evidence available." The collective was founded by three Belgian citizens: Isabelle Duchateau, a nurse who says she is "particularly concerned" about respect for patients' rights as well as "fair and uncorrupted" medical and scientific information; Stella André, a jurist of European law, who fears the rule of law and fundamental rights and freedoms "have been undermined since the beginning of the virus crisis"; and lastly, Benoit Clarembeau, a father of three children who says he is "anxious to assure them a future in a state of law."[11]

Notre Bon Droit is also contesting the legality of vaccine passports in France and has presented a similar case against the CST in Brussels. If the case produces the same initial result as in Namur, it will mean that a court in the EU's capital, where the Green Pass was first conceived, will have ruled that vaccine passports are illegal. As of early January, no ruling had been made.

These developments offer a glimmer of hope in a continent gone dark. But it is still only the faintest of glimmers. Even judicial obstructions to the vaccine passport can be quickly overturned, as the people of Spain learned in the late summer of 2021.

In August, the regional high court of Andalusia, in Southern Spain, ruled against the use of COVID passports to restrict access to public spaces. When the case reached Spain's Supreme Court, in mid-August, the court ratified the decision, becoming the first judicial authority in Europe to rule against the use of COVID passports to restrict access to public spaces.[12] But the ruling lasted only a month. On September 14, following a request from the regional government of Galicia, the Supreme Court decided that vaccine passports were, after all, a "suitable, necessary and proportionate" measure to prevent new infections in regions at high risk of contagion. By early December, eight of Spain's seventeen regions had made the certificate a condition of entry to certain spaces, including bars, restaurants, and hospitals.[13]

The lesson is clear: No one city, region or even nation can single-handedly stop vaccine passports from becoming a reality. But if enough people in enough countries mount a concerted campaign of opposition across all levels of society, anything is possible.

Time is of the essence, however. By the end of 2021, just about every nation in Europe had passed legislation making vaccine passports a precondition for entry to public places, including one of the last holdouts, England. On December 15, the United Kingdom's House of Commons, one of the world's oldest parliaments, passed the Boris Johnson government's "Plan B" legislation for England, which included the introduction of vaccine passports for nightclubs and large venues.[14] In the process, the Johnson government suffered its biggest backbench rebellion to date, but it was still able to pass the legislation, thanks to the support of the increasingly supine Labour Party.[15]

The legislation cleared the chamber despite the fact that vaccine passports clearly do not work, especially against a COVID-19 variant like Omicron that so easily evades the vaccines. What's more, mandatory COVID Passes contradict the advice of the UK Parliament's Public Administration and Constitutional Affairs Committee (PACAC) report into COVID-19 status certification, which concluded that the government could not make a solid scientific case in support of vaccine passports, and that they would be discriminatory.[16]

In the months preceding the vote, friends and family members in the UK told me, with characteristic British pride, that the hugely discriminatory policies and practices taking place across mainland Europe would never be allowed in a country as traditionally liberal and democratic as the UK. They were wrong, but only to an extent. On January 19, Boris Johnson took the world by surprise—or at least the world outside the UK—when he announced plans to lift almost all of the "Plan B" measures for England, including the COVID-19 certificate. In so doing it became the first so-called "liberal democracy" to emphatically reject the need for mandatory domestic COVID-19 status certification.

"The end of Covid passes in England is a MONUMENTAL victory for civil liberties & equality," wrote Silkie Carlo, director of the British civil liberties NGO Big Brother Watch. "What separates us from much of the covid-ID-managed West is the principled courage of every Brit who stood up when it mattered, against the odds, & our uniquely strong civil society."[17]

The policy U-turn was an act of political desperation by a government brought to its knees by an endless succession of corruption scandals. After so many of Boris Johnson's cabinet ministers as well as Johnson himself had been caught flouting their own COVID-19 rules and then lying about it, there was only one way for the Government to stay standing: to get rid of the rules. But it's touch and go whether it will be enough. As I am writing this, the media campaign against Johnson is intensifying, pretenders to the throne are sharpening their knives, and former cabinet ministers are calling on the PM to resign. By the time this book is published, Johnson could already be out of office. If so, his replacement could very quickly reverse policy once again and resurrect the restrictions. Alternatively, they might get rid of the restrictions Johnson left in place, such as the vaccine mandate for all NHS staff. For the moment, there is no way of knowing which way the wind will blow. As has been the case since the Brexit referendum of 2016, the UK is in a highly fluid situation.

Spreading the Hate

In the EU, meanwhile, the vaccine passports and mandates are encroaching inexorably into just about every facet of the economy and society. In the same week the UK dropped its "Plan B" restrictions, Austrian lawmakers approved Europe's first near-universal coronavirus vaccine mandate and Italy's government issued an edict banning people without the vaccine certificate from all retail premises except supermarkets, pharmacies, opticians, pet shops, and gas stations. With each new encroachment, the governments of Europe, with the European Commission leading the charge, drive the final nail deeper into the coffin of liberal democracy. Much the same is happening in Canada, Australia, New Zealand, and parts of the

United States. If we allow this to happen, we will go down in history as the generation that oversaw the end of liberty—and did nothing about it. When, in the future, our children and grandchildren ask us how democracy died, we will be able to borrow these words from Ernest Hemingway's *The Sun Also Rises* (on how bankruptcies unfold): "Two ways. Gradually, then suddenly."

None of this would have been possible without the assistance of the legacy media. One of the darkest, most Orwellian devices deployed by today's army of propagandists is the claim that people opposed to vaccine passports are depriving the rest of society of their freedoms. A perfect example of this was provided by veteran British journalist Andrew Neil who, on December 9, 2021, just days before the UK government's vaccine passport bill passed through parliament, published an article in the *Daily Mail* titled: "It's Time to Punish Britain's Five Million Vaccine Refuseniks: They Put Us All at Risk of More Restrictions. So Why Shouldn't We Curb Some of Their Freedoms?" In the article, Neil wrote:

> *As long as they can be numbered in the millions, the nation will remain unnecessarily vulnerable to the latest variant, meaning more lockdowns, more restrictions on our lives, more lost jobs, more failing business, less economic growth—all of which will follow the Government's introduction of its so-called Plan B of enhanced restrictions this week. . . .*
>
> *Under Plan B, vaccine passports will be required for entry to nightclubs and at major gatherings at large venues. It would not be difficult to extend them, French-style, to other public places, including restaurants, pubs and bars, and non-essential shops (even the unvaxxed need food and medicines!).*
>
> *It would give those of us who've done the right thing more protection and for those who've not, pause for thought.* [18]

Like many celebrities and high-ranking media figures, Neil paints vaccine passports as "a minor inconvenience," especially when "a new wave of the coronavirus pandemic is sweeping across the continent." What he doesn't mention is that Europe is already far and away the most vaccinated continent on the planet. It also has more vaccine passports per person than any other region.

Given that the current crop of COVID-19 vaccines is non-sterilizing and incredibly leaky, particularly against the Omicron variant, everyone in Europe, the UK included, could be forcefully vaccinated and the continent would still be vulnerable to the latest variant. Gibraltar—the most vaccinated place in the world—cancelled Christmas due to a surge in COVID cases. The entire eligible population of Gibraltar is vaccinated.

This is where the entire basis of Neil's argument collapses: The vaccine passports are not helping countries combat transmission of the virus and may actually be exacerbating it. How else to explain the fact that by the end of 2021 the EU, whose 27 Member States had been using vaccine passports to one degree or another for almost half a year, was once again ground zero for the COVID-19 pandemic?

Besides preparing the psychological ground for acceptance of the vaccine passport, the scapegoating of the unvaccinated serves another agenda: to shift the blame for the further ratcheting of restrictions, loss of freedoms, and the inevitable economic fallout that will follow from those who are truly responsible—the government; public health agencies; organizations such as the WHO, the World Economic Forum, and the Bill and Melinda Gates Foundation; and the corporations they represent—to the unvaccinated.

The ultimate goal is to transform the fear and frustration festering in people's psyches into anger and hatred for the "other," while deflecting attention away from those who are really driving this process. It is a perfect example of divide and conquer, and the stakes could not be higher.

This is the battle of our lives, for our lives. The world as we know it is crossing the Rubicon, and on the other side lies a dark, bleak future of unfettered government and corporate surveillance and control. If governments are able to complete the construction of the biosecurity state, they will have at their disposal unprecedented tools to shape, mold, and control the population. They will be able to decide exactly what new experimental gene therapy goes into our bodies and when. They will have the capacity to control just about every aspect of human behavior, expression, and thought while also tracking our every movement.

Anyone who tries to resist will be easily identified and tracked down. This is a vital point: In other times of tyranny, there was always the possibility for opponents of the regime to run, hide, and regroup, albeit at huge risk. In tomorrow's biosecurity state that will not be possible. In other words, if we fail to act now, it will be virtually impossible to act in the future.

We don't just risk losing our privacy and basic rights and freedoms, which generations of our forebears have fought so hard to attain—we risk losing our collective soul. As has happened so many times during the darkest episodes of history, the voices of power—often through mouthpieces in the legacy media—are urging people to see the "other" (in this case the unvaccinated) as the "enemy." Resentment is also rising among the unvaccinated towards the vaccinated.

The authorities want to pit one side against the other, but we must try to resist falling into this trap. Do not let fear turn to hate. Remember: Both the vaccinated and the unvaccinated are your friends and neighbors, your brothers and sisters. They are your mothers and fathers, your sons and daughters. They are your doctors and nurses, your teachers and students.

History has taught us, time and again, that any government that preaches hatred toward one group of people is always happy to shift the focus of that hatred to another group whenever it suits them. In circumstances such as this, when your government is committing evil, passivity is not an option; it just encourages more. As the Romanian-born American writer, political activist, Nobel laureate, and Holocaust survivor Elie Wiesel once wrote, "We must take sides. Neutrality helps the oppressor, never the victim. Silence encourages the tormentor, never the tormented."

Rising Resistance

One of the ironies of today's world is that most people comply in order to make the restrictions, privations, and crackdowns end, but their compliance means they never do. The good news is that more and more people are beginning to realize this, and not a moment too soon. Throughout Europe, the United States, Australia, and far beyond, small acts of resistance are taking place. The shopkeeper who insists on continuing to serve his unvaccinated customers despite the threat of government fines. The cinema owner who refuses to close her doors to unvaccinated film lovers. The doctor who continues to treat unvaccinated patients, despite government rules forbidding him from doing so.

Mass protest movements are also multiplying. By mid-December cities across France had witnessed twenty-two consecutive weekends of protest against the Macron government's COVID pass rules. The demonstrations have even extended to France's overseas territories. In late November, French authorities were forced to dispatch police reinforcements to Guadeloupe and impose a curfew on the Caribbean island after a week of "quasi-insurrectional arrest."[19] But the French government did postpone imposing a vaccine mandate on the island. It is a salutary lesson: The only way to stop governments from imposing more and more draconian restrictions on our lives is to stop complying with them—but to do so without resorting to violence.

In the Czech Republic, widespread demonstrations prompted the new center-right government to scrap a decree making COVID-19 vaccinations mandatory for essential workers and those over 60. As Reuters reported on January 19, the new Czech Government took the step in order to avoid "deepening fissures" in society. The decree had also failed to stop cases from reaching a new record high.[20]

Some cities in Italy have been rocked by so many demonstrations that the local authorities have resorted to banning them altogether, with the explicit support of Mario Draghi's technocratic government. On December 11, tens of thousands of people marched in Vienna in protest against the government's new COVID-19 restrictions, including home confinement orders for the unvaccinated and mandatory COVID-19 vaccines. A week later, protests took place in more than a dozen towns and cities, including Vienna, Innsbruck, Gmünd, and Leibnitz. Cities in Belgium, the Netherlands, Spain, and Croatia have also seen big protests.[21] In some countries in Eastern Europe, such as Romania, Albania, and Bulgaria, the majority of people, many of whom remember what life was like under communist rule, are still unvaccinated. It will be interesting to see how they react if the EU tries to force the vaccination on them.

Germany, the EU's most populous country and biggest economy, has seen wave after wave of demonstrations since the federal government announced plans, on November 30, 2021, to enforce mandatory vaccination. The German journalist Paul Schreyer, writing in the online news website *Multipolar Magazin* on December 17, likened the blossoming protest movement to the massive mobilizations of autumn 1989, which helped bring about the fall of the Berlin Wall:

> *Independent of each other and without central planning, weekly protests have been organized across numerous cities in a very short space of times. Over 50 German cities have been involved since last weekend: 8,000 demonstrators recently gathered in Hamburg, 3,000 each in Munich, Fürth, Magdeburg, Rostock and Cottbus, and 2,000 in Nuremberg, Reutlingen, Neumarkt, Freiburg, Aschaffenburg, Schweinfurt and Mannheim. In numerous other cities, the protests have grown to four-digit numbers in the past few days—in many cases, [the number of participants] has doubled compared to the previous week.*

> *Since the beginning of December, demonstrations have been taking place in German cities on an unprecedented scale against the corona policy and the planned mandatory vaccination. The number of protesters grows from week to week. A nationwide, decentralized movement is emerging. Local citizen committees, which are engaging in dialogue with elected city representatives at roundtables, could make the protest even more effective. At the moment, however, there is also a threat of escalation due to covertly staged acts of violence.*

> *Currently, an average of 0.5 to 2 percent of residents are demonstrating in the cities affected by the protest. According to the continuously updated, representative COSMO study by the University of Erfurt in cooperation with the Robert Koch Institute, as of December 3, 2021, 15 percent of the citizens surveyed*

> are "willing to take part in a demonstration against the restrictive measures." (PDF, p. 23) There is still considerable potential for the demonstrations to grow in size.[22]

There are also parallels with the tumultuous events of 1968. Some of those in the present demonstrations will be so-called "Achtundsechzige," former student protesters in 1968 who tried in vain to prevent the passing of the Emergency Powers Bill. The protests centered on the concern that the emergency law could give the government extraordinary powers. A combination of no effective opposition within parliament and waves of protest in neighboring countries (e.g., in France, where riots almost led to the toppling of the government in May 1968) fueled the debate across the country.

Though the protests could be viewed as specifically German, with a younger generation railing against the Nazi past of their parents' generation, the target was the perceived authoritarianism of a government being handed back emergency powers by the Allied Control Council. Despite its reputation as a law-abiding, orderly society, post-war Germany is no stranger to protest when its people fear its government is overstepping the mark. That is precisely what is happening today.

On January 3, 2022, an estimated 1,390 towns and cities took part in what was dubbed "a Monday walk," in direct defiance of the government's latest lockdown orders, according to the organizers' Telegram channel. The protest movement bears echoes of the Monday demonstrations that took place against the government of the German Democratic Republic (GDR) in towns and cities across East Germany between 1989 and 1991.[23]

"The government is concerned about the decentralized actions," reported Die Welt. "Against the NATO build-up, the Iraq war or greenhouse gas emissions, far larger protest marches have already formed than are currently taking place against the Corona policy. But never before in the history of the Federal Republic have there been demonstrations that are more widespread than in the last few weeks."[24]

As the movement grows, the government, with the help of the legacy media, both in Germany and abroad, is trying to demonize all protesters. One popular strategy, already trialed in Italy and France, is to paint them all with the broad brush of neo-Nazism, which in Germany has a particularly powerful effect. In the subheading of its December 14 article, "Anti-Corona Protests Escalate, Riots in Several German Cities," the *Jerusalem Post* reported that "anti-vaccination activists and right-wing extremists are merging into a homogeneous mass":

> *German Interior Minister Nancy Faeser lamented an increasing propensity to violence and radicalization at demonstrations against the Corona measures. "The propensity to violence is increasing," Faeser stated on her Twitter account:*
>
>> *"Many lateral thinkers are becoming more radical. Threats and intimidation are completely unacceptable! We must step up efforts for social cohesion and overcome the attempts at division by anti-democratic forces."[25]*

Although it is true that far-right groups have played a role in Germany's antivaccine passport movement, to portray everyone who opposes the government's increasingly draconian policies as extremist is absurd, especially given that roughly one out of every four adults is still unvaccinated. It is also farcical to hear the Minister of Interior of a government that has imposed Europe's second "lockdown of the unvaccinated" talk about the need for social cohesion. Given the increasing number and size of the protests sweeping Germany, it seems that more and more people are seeing through it. According to Schreyer, the government's strategy of smearing the protests in a bid to prevent them from reaching a critical mass appears to be failing:

> *The legacy media have lost too much trust . . . for their reporting to penetrate effectively. In the absence of alternatives, attempts are still being made to demonize and marginalize the demonstrators as dangerous, confused people or right-wing extremists. Almost no comment from federal and state politicians on the protests comes without the words "radicalized" and "violence." This seems all the stranger as the demonstrations have so far been predominantly peaceful.*

One of the main tools the protesters have used to organize demonstrations and to share information is the Telegram messaging service. But in mid-January the German government threatened to ban the service altogether if it continued to be used in this way. "We cannot rule this out," said Faeser. "A shutdown would be grave and clearly a last resort. All other options must be exhausted first." As *The Independent* reported at the time, "Germany is not alone in potentially seeking controls on Telegram. Bans and regulations exist in a variety of countries, from China to India and Russia"—three countries that are not exactly famed for their respect for freedom of speech.[26] But this, alas, is the direction in which we appear to be heading in Europe.

Germany's new chancellor, Olaf Scholz, who took over from Angela Merkel in November 2021, has responded to the burgeoning protest movement with tougher and tougher language.

"We must counter threats with all severity. I want to keep the country together. And so, I am also the chancellor of the unvaccinated," he said in mid-December. The last sentence was hardly comforting given that days earlier Scholz had said: "For my government there are no more red lines in everything that has to be done. There is nothing we can rule out."[27]

While Germany's new president was feigning concern for the unvaccinated, the prime minister of France, Jean Castex, had a surprise of his own up his sleeve. As of mid-February 2022, negative test results would no longer suffice for anyone over 16 to qualify for the "pass sanitaire," which would essentially become a "pass vaccinal." Unless you are fully vaccinated, which according to the new rules will mean taking a booster shot within four months of your last shot, or you can prove you have had an infection in the past four months if you are over 18 (down from six months), you will not be able to access most public spaces.

With the new rules, France will become the first (but presumably not the last) EU Member State to completely abandon negative PCR test results in its vaccine passport legislation as well as shorten the length of time infection-acquired immunity buys you. Germany has also reduced the validity of the recovery certificates from six to three months and is urging the EU to do the same in its Green Pass legislation.[28] The fact this is happening while evidence continues to mount that the protection provided by naturally acquired immunity is both broader and longer-lasting than vaccine-derived immunity is yet more proof that these draconian measures have little to do with public health.

"We intend to put the pressure on the unvaccinated," said Castex, as if they hadn't been doing just that for the preceding five months.[29] A few weeks later, French President Emmanuel Macron stoked divisions even further by pledging to "piss off the unvaccinated" (*emmerder les non-vaccinés*), whom he apparently blames for France's record COVID-19 case numbers.[30] The abrupt rewriting of the rules, to turn the screws even tighter on the country's millions of unvaccinated citizens, should serve as a wake-up call for all French citizens who have the slightest regard for *liberté, fraternité*, and *egalité*—precious little of which will remain in the digital dystopia being rushed into existence.

America: The Last Stand?

Here's an interesting paradox: The country that produced most of the companies and technologies that are facilitating the march toward a digital dictatorship, the United States of America, could also end up being the last bastion of freedom. There are three main reasons for this: First, the constitutional checks and balances embedded within the US system of governance make it much harder to bulldoze into law legislation that threatens basic rights and liberties, as has happened in the EU. Second, the tensions between state rights and federal power have limited the federal government's ability to impose nationwide vaccine mandates. And third, individual liberty is far and away the most cherished political principle in the country, for better or worse, and one that is explicitly protected by the country's constitution.

Unlike in Europe, Australia, and New Zealand, vaccine mandates or passports have not been implemented across the board, despite the best efforts of the Biden administration. On November 4, 2021, the Biden administration ordered federal contractors, employees of businesses with 100 employees or more, and certain health care employees to show proof of full COVID-19 vaccination, or get weekly COVID-19 testing, by January 4, 2022. But as recent developments in the country have shown, it is a lot easier to draw up a vaccine mandate than it is to enforce it.[31]

The mandates got strong pushback straight away. Entire sections of COVID-19 vaccine requirements have been temporarily blocked, as lawsuits challenging the mandates have proliferated. On November 12, the US Court of Appeals for the Fifth Circuit ordered the Occupational Safety and Health Administration (OSHA) to "take no steps to implement or enforce the Mandate until further court order." This effectively put on hold COVID-19 vaccination and testing requirements for companies with 100 employees or more, which affects around 84 million US workers.

Biden's executive order requiring contractors to ensure their workers are vaccinated against COVID and enforcing mask and social distancing policies has also met stiff opposition. So, too, has the mandate for health care workers to get vaccinated. Some of the court-imposed restrictions on the mandates had been lifted by the end of 2021, but the final decision will probably lie with the judges of the country's most powerful court. As the attorney, legal scholar, writer, commentator, and legal analyst Jonathan Turley notes, "all of these mandates are on course for a showdown in the Supreme Court where three (of the nine) justices have already expressed skepticism over the mandates:"

> *On October 29, 2021, three Supreme Court justices dissented in a case where they felt review should have been granted. Justices Gorsuch, Thomas, and Alito raised questions over whether past deference on the pandemic is warranted and warned that the "compelling interest" recognized in such past cases "cannot qualify as such forever."*
>
> *Over the last year, courts have remained highly deferential. However, the three justices previously noted that "if human nature and history teach us anything, it is that civil liberties face grave risks when governments proclaim indefinite states of emergency."[32]*

As the impasse continues, the legal disparities among states and municipalities continue to grow. In November 2021, a federal court in Louisiana blocked President Biden's vaccine mandate for health care workers. As a result, many hospitals suspended their vaccine requirements, to ease severe labor shortages, while others left them in place. As the *Wall Street Journal* noted, thousands of nurses have left the industry or lost their jobs rather than get vaccinated:

> As of September, 30 percent of workers at more than 2,000 hospitals across the country surveyed by the Centers for Disease Control and Prevention were unvaccinated.
>
> "It's been a mass exodus, and a lot of people in the health care industry are willing to go and shop around," said Wade Symons, an employee-benefits lawyer and head of consulting firm Mercer's US regulatory practice. "If you get certain health care facilities that don't require it, those could be a magnet for those people who don't want the vaccine. They'll probably have an easier time attracting labor."[33]

To add to the chaos, on December 15, 2021, the New Orleans–based US Fifth Circuit Court of Appeals lifted a nationwide ban against the federal government's vaccine mandate for health care workers, leaving it in place only in the 14 states that had collectively sued in federal court, in Louisiana and 10 other states where the mandate was blocked by a separate November 29 ruling. As a result, many of the hospitals in the 26 states where the mandate was reinstated that had dropped their vaccine requirements would now have to reinstate them, unless of course another injunction was granted. On January 14, the U.S. Supreme weighed in on the matter, temporarily blocking the OSHA rule and upholding the vaccine mandates for most healthcare workers.

Another irony is that three of the United States' most important weaknesses when it came to mounting a united, coordinated response to the pandemic—its decentralized system of government, the abject incompetence and corruption of its public health agencies, and its disjointed, largely private, for-profit health care system—are now preventing it from hurtling headlong into a biomedical dictatorship. Unlike Brussels, Washington cannot order the 50 states of the Union to adopt vaccine mandates—at least not yet!

That is likely to get even harder as more and more evidence emerges confirming the vaccines' even lower efficacy at preventing transmission of the Omicron variant. As Biden himself conceded in the final week of 2021, "there is no federal solution to the pandemic."[34] Of course, there could have been a federal solution, but it would have required more honest public messaging, better preparedness, and a broader strategy involving more measures than just vaccine mandates and scapegoating of the unvaccinated. There is also little sign of Washington being able to develop and impose a centralized vaccine passport system for the whole country, at least not without sparking civil war.

And that is a good thing. It has spared large swathes of the country the dark, discriminatory, dangerous policies that are radically reconfiguring societies across Europe and other parts of the globe. That said, many parts of the United States *have* installed vaccine passport systems and mandates, albeit at a local or state level.

In some places, the measures adopted are at least on par with those in Europe. On December 6, 2021, New York City Mayor Bill de Blasio demanded that all children aged 5 to 11 show proof of vaccination to access "public indoor activities." Yet despite all of its vaccine mandates and vaccine passport system, New York was still struggling to contain the virus at the end of 2021. The state has one of the highest vaccination rates among the most populous states in the United States but between early December and early January was registering single-day records for positive COVID cases almost every day.[35]

Basta Ya!

Almost all of the vaccine passport mandates and vaccine systems being rolled out in the United States are in Democratic states, where the governing class and its voters pride themselves on their devotion to diversity, tolerance, and social justice. That same governing class, in its obeisance to corporate power, is installing a new system of discrimination and segregation that, if not stopped, will prove to be far more efficient at excluding second-class citizens from society than even the racial segregation policies of the past century.

Yet many Democratic supporters look on and applaud, or at least nod their heads in quiet approval. As the British author Paul Kingsnorth notes, COVID has revealed the authoritarian streak that lies beneath so many people, and which always emerges in fearful times:

> *In the last month alone, I have watched media commentators calling for censorship of their political opponents, philosophy professors justifying mass internment, and human rights lobby groups remaining silent about "vaccine passports." I have watched much of the political Left transition openly into the authoritarian movement it probably always was, and countless "liberals" campaigning against liberty. As freedom after freedom has been taken away, I have watched intellectual after intellectual justify it all.* [36]

It is time to say "*Basta ya!*" (enough already). This is not about whether you have been vaccinated or not, or how many times you have been vaccinated. It is about whether you are willing to give up all agency over your own life for a vaccine that doesn't prevent transmission.

This is a one-time deal we are (not really) being offered. For the vast majority of us who make up the lower and middle strata of the economic and social classes, it is a rotten deal. We are being told to give up virtually everything that matters—our freedom to associate with whomever we choose, to move around (not just from country to country but within our own countries and, if recent developments in Italy are any indication, within our own cities), to express ourselves freely, to inform and think for ourselves, to protest government corruption, abuse, or overreach, to decide for ourselves what experimental medical products go into our bodies, to work—in return for virtually nothing.

For governments and national security agencies, the benefits of the digital dictatorship are clear: expanded power and control at a time when economic conditions are about to get unimaginably worse for the vast majority of the population. For big tech companies, it will create new opportunities to amass even more data over our lives, which they will then be able to transform into even more revenues and profits. For big pharma, the biosecurity state provides the perfect business model. Vaccine mandates ensure continuous demand for the products they produce, no matter how substandard or unsafe they may be.

Before the COVID-19 pandemic Moderna was close to collapse as safety concerns and other reservations about its mRNA delivery system imperiled its entire product pipeline. As of mid-January 2022, its share price was worth more than five times its value in March 2020 despite having fallen 65 percent from a record high it registered in September 2021. During a panel discussion organized by the World Economic Forum in January 2022, CEO Stéphane Bancel said his company is now working on a combined booster vaccination for COVID-19, influenza, and RSV.[37] In the same week, Bill Gates issued yet another warning that the world was facing pandemics even more dangerous than COVID-19 and called on governments to invest yet more money in the vaccine technologies in which he, through his foundation, is heavily invested.[38] In the meantime, we ignore most other key areas of public health policy, including early outpatient treatment, ventilation, and preventive health measures. As my colleague at the economic and finance blog Naked Capitalism, Yves Smith, wrote in her article, "Covid: The Narrative Is Crumbling," the United States "should be ashamed that third world countries are doing better by sending diagnosis and treatment kits to citizens, with care packs including thermometers, blood oximeters, test kits, zinc, Vitamin C, Vitamin D, OTC meds for fever, and sometimes the I drug."[39]

For the vast majority of the world's population, this deal does not offer any real benefits, just drawbacks, privations, and punishments, which is probably why we are not being consulted on or even informed of its terms and conditions. Yet the governments of ostensibly democratic nations still need the tacit consent of the majority, even as they try to snuff out what remains of our basic rights and freedoms.

Before it is too late, which will be sooner rather than later, we need to ask ourselves one simple question: Where is my red line? For many people, their red line is the mass vaccination of healthy children, who are at less risk from the virus than adults and whose young bodies will needlessly be exposed to the risk of the as-yet unknown long-term side effects of the vaccines.

Where is yours? Forced vaccination? A booster shot every two or three months? Unfettered surveillance? Indefinite detention for those who disobey? Total censorship of social media? Digital checkpoints everywhere you go? All for upholding the use of leaky vaccines that don't even protect against transmission of the Delta variant and which appear to be even leakier against Omicron.

Wherever your red line may be, the chances are that by the time it is crossed, it will already be too late to mount a resistance. Day by day, hour by hour, the digital control grid is tightening around us while our democratically elected governments are carrying out a wholesale bonfire of our basic rights and freedoms.

But there is still a brief window of time in which the populations of the world's liberal democracies—vaccinated and unvaccinated— can unite to stop this madness from becoming permanent, turn back the clock, and reclaim agency over our lives. Enough is enough!

ACKNOWLEDGMENTS

FIRST AND FOREMOST, I would like to thank my beloved wife, Alaisita, without whom I would not have been able to write this book. She kept me well fed, entertained, and on an even keel, and occasionally accompanied me down some pretty dark tunnels during these intense months of writing. I also owe an immense debt of gratitude to Wolf Richter, of the San Francisco–based business and financial website Wolf Street, for giving me a place to write and for teaching me so much about finance and economics as well as the importance of using and understanding raw data.

I am also hugely grateful to Yves Smith, Lambert Strether, and Jerry-Lynn Scofield at *Naked Capitalism* for making me feel part of their team and giving me editorial freedom to cover issues that many publishers dare not touch, including the dark side of vaccine passports. I also owe a big thank you to Larisa Tatge and Brianne Goodspeed for doing such a great job on the editing, and to Margo Baldwin for having the courage to publish this book.

Closer to home, my father, as always, has been a rock of support for both myself and my wife throughout this pandemic, despite living over 1,000 miles away. Thanks also to my mother for always being there and keeping me abreast of family news, and my mother-in-law, Sylvia, for encouraging me to start writing my own articles almost a decade ago. Lastly, a quick shout out to Gus, Gerard, and Dom for providing brief moments of distraction from the writing process as well as listening, stoically, to my odd, occasional rant, and Mimi for keeping me constantly abreast of the latest developments in Central Europe.

NOTES

Introduction

1. Glenn Greenwald, "I Oppose Them for the Same Reasons I Opposed the War on Terror," Bari Weiss, ed. "Vaccine Mandates: The End of Covid? Or the Beginning of Tyranny?," *Common Sense*, September 22, 2021, https://bariweiss.substack.com/p/vaccine-mandates-the-end-of-covid.

2. Good Morning Britain, "'Vaccination, in the End, Will Be Your Route to Liberty,' Says Tony Blair," interview by Piers Morgan and Susanna Reid with Tony Blair, YouTube video, 14:31, January 6, 2021, https://www.youtube.com/watch?v=QA9Ms5-D-f0.

3. Kristel Teyras, "How Digital ID Can Help Citizens Access Government Services from Anywhere," *Thales*, last updated December 1, 2021, https://dis-blog.thalesgroup.com/identity-biometric-solutions/2021/07/27/how-digital-id-can-help-citizens-access-government-services-from-anywhere.

4. Mathieu Pollet, "Blockchain Might Be the Solution to the Digital Identity Hurdle," *EURACTIV France*, September 8, 2021, https://www.euractiv.com/section/digital/news/blockchain-might-be-the-solution-to-the-digital-identity-hurdle.

5. "The European Payments Initiative: Laying the Infrastructure for Europe's Super Payments App," *PYMNTS*, September 14, 2021, https://www.pymnts.com/news/payment-methods/2021/the-european-payments-initiative-laying-the-infrastructure-for-europes-super-payments-app.

6. "#CashFridays," *The Solari Report*, July 2, 2021, https://home.solari.com/cash-friday/.

7. Marianne Guenot, "Israel's Vaccine Pass Will Expire 6 Months after the 2nd Dose, Meaning People Will Need Booster Shots to Keep Going to Restaurants and Bars," *Business Insider*, September 1, 2021, https://www.businessinsider.com/israel-vaccine-pass-to-expire-after-6-months-booster-shots-2021-9.

8. Reuters, "Israel Approves 4th Covid Vaccine Dose for People 60 and Over," *New York Times*, January 2, 2022, https://www.nytimes.com/video/world/middleeast/100000008143010/israel-covid-vaccine-booster.html.

9. "COVID-19: Italy Makes Vaccine Passport Compulsory—Workers Can Be Fined and Suspended without Pay," *Sky News*, September 17, 2021, https://news.sky.com/story/covid-19-italy-makes-vaccine-passport-compulsory-workers-can-be-fined-and-suspended-without-pay-12410130.

10. Kaia Hubbard, "24 States Threaten Legal Action Against Biden's Vaccine Mandate," *US News and World Report*, September 16, 2021, https://www

.usnews.com/news/health-news/articles/2021-09-16/24-states-threaten
-legal-action-against-bidens-vaccine-mandate.

11. Kevin Breuninger and Spencer Kimball, "Businesses, Republican States Ask
Supreme Court to Halt Biden Vaccine and Testing Mandate," CNBC,
updated December 20, 2021, https://www.cnbc.com/2021/12/20/covid
-news-supreme-court-asked-to-halt-biden-vaccine-and-testing-mandate.html.

12. Reuters and The Associated Press, "Municipal Workers Protest Against N.Y.C.
Vaccine Mandate," *New York Times*, October 25, 2021, https://www.nytimes
.com/video/us/100000008043411/nyc-covid-vaccine-mandate-protest.html.

13. Álvaro Soto, "El Supremo tumba el pasaporte covid para entrar en el ocio
nocturno" [The Supreme Court Knocks Down the COVID Passport to
Enter the Nightlife], *El Correo*, August 18, 2021, https://www.elcorreo.com
/sociedad/salud/supremo-tumba-pasaporte-20210818170045-ntrc.html.

14. "PM Speech to the UN General Assembly: 24 September 2019," Gov.UK,
September 25, 2019, https://www.gov.uk/government/speeches/pm-speech
-to-the-un-general-assembly-24-september-2019.

15. AFP/Reuters, "British Vaccine Experts Do Not Recommend Jab for Healthy
12–15s," *RTÉ*, September 3, 2021, https://www.rte.ie/news/coronavirus
/2021/0903/1244452-coronavirus-global.

Chapter 1: Logical Insanity

1. Barbara Jacquelyn Sahakian et al., "Vaccine Passports: Why They Are Good for
Society," *The Conversation*, May 13, 2021, https://theconversation.com
/vaccine-passports-why-they-are-good-for-society-160419.

2. Mira Patel, "From Smallpox to COVID-19: The History of Vaccine Passports
and How It Impacts International Relations," *The Indian Express*, June 4, 2021,
https://indianexpress.com/article/research/from-smallpox-to-covid-19
-the-history-of-vaccine-passports-and-how-it-impacts-international
-relations-7274871.

3. Philippa Roxby and Nick Triggle, "Scientists Not Backing COVID Jabs for
12- to 15-Year-Olds," *BBC News*, September 3, 2021, https://www.bbc.com
/news/health-58438669.

4. Sarah Tanveer et al., "Transparency of COVID-19 Vaccine Trials: Decisions
without Data," *BMJ Evidence-Based Medicine*, August 9, 2021, doi:10.1136
/bmjebm-2021-111735.

5. Jenna Greene, "Wait What? FDA Wants 55 Years to Process FOIA Request over
Vaccine Data," *Reuters*, November 18, 2021, https://www.reuters.com/legal
/government/wait-what-fda-wants-55-years-process-foia-request-over
-vaccine-data-2021-11-18/.

6. Jenna Greene, "'Paramount importance': Judge Orders FDA to Hasten Release
of Pfizer Vaccine Docs," *Reuters*, January 7, 2022, https://www.reuters.com
/legal/government/paramount-importance-judge-orders-fda-hasten-release
-pfizer-vaccine-docs-2022-01-07.

7. Kasen K. Riemersma et al., "Vaccinated and Unvaccinated Individuals Have
Similar Viral Loads in Communities with a High Prevalence of the

SARS-CoV-2 Delta Variant," *medRxiv*, July 31, 2021, doi:10.1101/2021.07
.31.21261387v1.

8. Laurel Wamsley, "Vaccinated People with Breakthrough Infections Can
Spread the Delta Variant, CDC Says," *NPR News*, July 30, 2021, https://
www.npr.org/sections/coronavirus-live-updates/2021/07/30/1022867219
/cdc-study-provincetown-delta-vaccinated-breakthrough-mask-guidance.

9. Ricardo Alonso-Zaldivar, "Questioning a Catchphrase: 'Pandemic of the
Unvaccinated,'" *AP News*, September 1, 2021, https://apnews.com/article
/health-pandemics-coronavirus-pandemic-9845c7257300ff6546c
20489e642a1ea.

10. Hannah Kuchler and John Burn-Murdoch, "Are Vaccines Becoming Less
Effective at Preventing Covid Infection?," *Financial Times*, August 19, 2021,
https://www.ft.com/content/49641651-e10a-45f6-a7cc-8b8c7b7a9710.

11. "Vaccinations in United Kingdom," Gov.UK, last updated September 1, 2021,
https://coronavirus.data.gov.uk/details/vaccinations.

12. "Daily Number of Patients in Hospital with Coronavirus (COVID-19) in the
United Kingdom (UK)," *Statista*, last updated November 1, 2021, https://
www.statista.com/statistics/1190423/hospital-cases-due-to-covid-19
-in-the-uk; "Daily Number of Coronavirus (COVID-19) Patients in
Mechanical Ventilation Beds in the United Kingdom (UK)," *Statista*, last
updated November 1, 2021, https://www.statista.com/statistics/1190451
/covid-19-patients-on-ventilators-in-the-uk.

13. Crown, "COVID-19 Vaccine Surveillance Report, Week 36," Public Health
England, September 9, 2021, https://assets.publishing.service.gov.uk
/government/uploads/system/uploads/attachment_data/file/1016465
/Vaccine_surveillance_report_-_week_36.pdf: 15.

14. Meredith Wadman, "A Grim Warning from Israel: Vaccination Blunts, but
Does Not Defeat Delta," *Science*, August 16, 2021, https://www.science.org
/content/article/grim-warning-israel-vaccination-blunts-does-not-defeat-delta.

15. Andrew Solender, "CDC Director Says Coronavirus Vaccines Less Effective
for Delta but Still Prevent Severe Infection," *Forbes*, August 18, 2021, https://
www.forbes.com/sites/andrewsolender/2021/08/18/cdc-director-says
-coronavirus-vaccines-less-effective-for-delta-but-still-prevent-severe-infection.

16. S. V. Subramanian and Akhil Kumar, "Increases in COVID-19 Are Unrelated
to Levels of Vaccination across 68 Countries and 2947 Counties in the United
States," *European Journal of Epidemiology* 36 (September 2021), 1237–40,
doi:10.1007/s10654-021-00808-7.

17. Channel 4 News (@Channel4News), "'Herd immunity is not a possibility'
because the Delta variant 'still infects vaccinated individuals'. Professor Sir
Andrew Pollard, director of the Oxford Vaccine Group, says there is
nothing . . .," August 10, 2021, 6:27 AM, https://twitter.com/channel4news
/status/1425086490002997248.

18. Jef Akst, "Omicron Appears to Evade Vaccines Better Than Other Variants," *The
Scientist*, December 14, 2021, https://www.the-scientist.com/news-opinion
/omicron-appears-to-evade-vaccines-better-than-other-variants-69525.

Notes

19. Stephanie Nolan, "Most of the World's Vaccines Likely Won't Prevent Infection from Omicron," *New York Times*, updated December 21, 2021, https://www.nytimes.com/2021/12/19/health/omicron-vaccines -efficacy.html.
20. Madeline Holcombe, "It May Take 'Many, Many' More Vaccine Mandates to End the COVID-19 Pandemic, Fauci Says," *CNN Health*, September 14, 2021, https://edition.cnn.com/2021/09/13/health/us-coronavirus-monday /index.html.
21. Alek Korab, "Dr. Fauci Just Said This about Your 'Individual Freedom,'" *Yahoo Life*, October 7, 2021, https://www.yahoo.com/lifestyle/dr-fauci-just-said -individual-121519548.html.
22. Vinay Prasad, "Vaccine Effectiveness (Against Infection Not Severe Disease) Goes Down the Drain," *Vinay Prasad's Observations and Thoughts* (blog), January 9, 2022, https://vinayprasadmdmph.substack.com/p/vaccine -effectiveness-goes-down-the.
23. Vinay Prasad, "Vaccine Effectiveness Goes Down the Drain."
24. Meredith Wadman, "Having SARS-CoV-2 Once Confers Much Greater Immunity than a Vaccine—but Vaccination Remains Vital," *Science*, August 26, 2921, doi:10.1126/science.abm1207.
25. Catherine H. Bozio et al., "Laboratory-Confirmed COVID-19 among Adults Hospitalized with COVID-19–Like Illness with Infection-Induced or mRNA Vaccine-Induced SARS-CoV-2 Immunity—Nine States, January–September 2021," *Morbidity and Mortality Weekly Report* 70, no. 44 (November 2021), 1539–44, doi:10.15585/mmwr.mm7044e1.
26. "COVID Certificate Adapted Amid Special Vaccination Drive," swissinfo.ch, November 3, 2021, https://www.swissinfo.ch/eng/covid-certificate-and -jabs/47080616.
27. Phil Galewitz, "Health Experts Worry CDC's Covid Vaccination Rates Appear Inflated," *KHN*, December 9, 2021, https://khn.org/news/article /cdc-senior-covid-vaccination-rates-appear-inflated.
28. Crown, "COVID-19 Vaccine Surveillance Report, Week 49," Public Health England, December 9, 2021, https://assets.publishing.service.gov.uk /government/uploads/system/uploads/attachment_data/file/1039677 /Vaccine_surveillance_report_-_week_49.pdf.
29. Charlotte Becquart, "Boardmasters: Nearly 5000 COVID Cases Potentially Linked to Festival So Far," *Cornwall News*, August 23, 2021, https://www .cornwalllive.com/news/cornwall-news/boardmasters-nearly-5000-covid -cases-5821841.
30. Robert Towney, "Harvard Business School Temporarily Moves Some MBA Classes Online to Curb COVID Outbreak," CNBC, September 27, 2021, https://www.cnbc.com/2021/09/27/harvard-business-school-temporarily -moves-some-mba-classes-online-to-curb-covid-outbreak.html.
31. Jeremy Fugleberg, "This South Dakota Nursing Home Was 100% Vaccinated. COVID-19 Broke Through Anyway. Here's How," *Grand Forks Herald*, July 30, 2021, https://www.grandforksherald.com/newsmd/coronavirus

/7133868-This-South-Dakota-nursing-home-was-100-vaccinated.
-COVID-19-broke-through-anyway.-Heres-how.

32. Jonathan Beale and Hazel Shearing, "HMS Queen Elizabeth: COVID
Outbreak on Navy Flagship," BBC News, July 14, 2021, https://www.bbc
.com/news/uk-57830617.

33. Reuters, "Lithuanian Hospitals Stop Accepting Non-urgent Patients amid
COVID-19 Surge," *Reuters*, October 15, 2021, https://www.reuters.com
/world/europe/lithuanian-hospitals-stop-accepting-non-urgent-patients
-amid-covid-19-surge-2021-10-15.

34. Aayushi Pratap, "Pfizer Expects $33.5 Billion in Vaccine Revenue in 2021,"
Forbes, July 28, 2021, https://www.forbes.com/sites/aayushipratap/2021
/07/28/pfizer-expects-335-billion-in-vaccine-revenue-in-2021.

35. Peter Loftus and Matt Grossman, "Moderna Turns First Profit, Boosted by Its
COVID-19 Vaccine," *Wall Street Journal*, May 6, 2021, https://www.wsj
.com/articles/moderna-turns-first-ever-profit-boosted-by-its-covid-19
-vaccine-11620302289.

36. Thomas Saunders, "COVID Vaccine: 111,000 NHS Workers Are Still
Unvaccinated and Yet to Receive a Single Dose," *iNews*, October 5, 2021,
https://inews.co.uk/news/health/covid-vaccine-nhs-workers-havent-had
-jab-uk-mandatory-vaccination-1233173.

37. William Philip et al., "Open Letter from Christian Leaders to the Prime
Minister Concerning Vaccine Passport Proposals," *Christian Leaders—
Vaccine Passport Letters*, August 2021, https://vaccinepassportletter
.wordpress.com.

Chapter 2: Your Body, Their Choice

1. "The Nuremberg Code (1947)," *British Medical Journal* 313, no. 7070
(December 7, 1996): 1448, https://media.tghn.org/medialibrary/2011/04
/BMJ_No_7070_Volume_313_The_Nuremberg_Code.pdf.

2. "Bodily Autonomy: Busting 7 Myths That Undermine Individual Rights and
Freedoms," *United Nations Population Fund*, April 14, 2021, https://www
.unfpa.org/news/bodily-autonomy-busting-7-myths-undermine-individual
-rights-and-freedoms.

3. Spencer Kimball, "Federal Appeals Court Calls Biden Vaccine Mandate 'Fatally
Flawed' and 'Staggeringly Overbroad,'" *CNBC*, November 13, 2021, https://
www.cnbc.com/2021/11/13/federal-appeals-court-calls-biden-vaccine
-mandate-fatally-flawed-and-staggeringly-overbroad-.html.

4. Amy Howe, "Fractured Court Blocks Vaccine-or-Test Requirement for Large
Workplaces but Green-lights Vaccine Mandate for Health Care Workers,"
SCOTUSblog (blog), January 13, 2022, https://www.scotusblog.com/2022
/01/fractured-court-blocks-vaccine-or-test-requirement-for-large-workplaces
-but-green-lights-vaccine-mandate-for-health-care-workers.

5. Katie Gravagna et al., "Global Assessment of National Mandatory Vaccination
Policies and Consequences of Non-compliance," *Vaccine* 38, no. 49 (November 2020): 7865–73, doi:10.1016/j.vaccine.2020.09.063.

6. Steven Nelson, "Joe Biden Says He Won't Mandate Getting COVID-19 Vaccine, Wearing Masks," *New York Post*, December 4, 2020, https://nypost.com/2020/12/04/biden-wont-mandate-getting-covid-19-vaccine-wearing-masks.

7. Charles Lipson, "The Deep Politics of Vaccine Mandates," *Real Clear Politics*, September 15, 2021, https://www.realclearpolitics.com/articles/2021/09/15/the_deep_politics_of_vaccine_mandates_146408.html.

8. Philip Krause et al., "Considerations in Boosting COVID-19 Vaccine Immune Responses," *The Lancet* 398, no. 10308 (October 9, 2021): 1377–80, doi:10.1016/S0140-6736(21)02046-8.

9. Irina Anghel, "Frequent Boosters Spur Warning on Immune Response," *Bloomberg*, January 11, 2022, https://www.bloomberg.com/news/articles/2022-01-11/repeat-booster-shots-risk-overloading-immune-system-ema-says.

10. Angela Giuffrida, "Italy to Tighten Covid Rules for Unvaccinated with 'Super Green Pass,'" *The Guardian*, November 24, 2021, https://www.theguardian.com/world/2021/nov/24/italy-poised-to-tighten-rules-for-unvaccinated-with-super-green-pass.

11. Thomas Fazi, "Italy's Vaccine Passport Power Grab," *UnHerd*, September 29, 2021, https://unherd.com/2021/09/italys-cynical-plan-for-vaccine-passports.

12. Erick Valdés, *Biolaw: Origins, Doctrine and Juridical Applications on the Biosciences* (Cham, Switzerland: Springer, 2021).

13. "Declaration of Helsinki," *Wikipedia*, last modified November 4, 2021, https://en.wikipedia.org/wiki/Declaration_of_Helsinki.

14. "Right to Integrity of the Person," *European Commission*, last accessed November 17, 2021, https://ec.europa.eu/info/aid-development-cooperation-fundamental-rights/your-rights-eu/know-your-rights/dignity/right-integrity-person_en.

15. "*NEK veröffentlicht Zusammenfassung, Empfehlungen und Medienmitteilung zur Covid-19-Impfung*" [NEK Publishes Summary, Recommendations and Media Release on COVID-19 Vaccination], National Ethics Committee in the Field of Human Medicine NEK, December 2, 2021, https://www.nek-cne.admin.ch/de/ueber-uns/news/news-details/nek-veroeffentlicht-zusammenfassung-empfehlungen-und-medienmitteilung-zur-covid-19-impfung.

16. Sarah Toy, "Why Some Healthcare Workers Would Rather Lose Their Jobs Than Get Vaccinated," *The Wall Street Journal*, October 22, 2021, https://www.wsj.com/articles/covid-19-vaccinations-healthcare-workers-refuse-risk-jobs-11634915929.

17. Meredith Wadman, "Having SARS-CoV-2 Once Confers Much Greater Immunity Than a Vaccine—but Vaccination Remains Vital," *Science* August 26, 2021, https://www.science.org/content/article/having-sars-cov-2-once-confers-much-greater-immunity-vaccine-vaccination-remains-vital.

18. Richard Raycraft, "Don't Expect EI If You Lose Your Job for Not Being Vaccinated, Minister Says," CBC News, October 21, 2021, https://www.cbc.ca/news/politics/ei-vax-status-1.6220287.

19. Eva Karene Bartlett, @EvaKBartlett, "Excellent points by Canadian criminal defence lawyer, Nicholas Wansbutter, arguing vaccine passports would

be anti-consent, and that the case law makes clear it is an assault. https://youtube.com/watch?v=9TsAQs92wto" Twitter post, August 23, 2021, 5:40 AM, https://twitter.com/EvaKBartlett/status/1429785630674989062.

20. Aaron Kheriaty, "The University of California Has Put Me on Leave for Challenging Their Vaccine Mandate," *Brownstone*, October 7, 2021, https://brownstone.org/articles/the-university-of-california-has-put-me-on-leave-for-challenging-their-vaccine-mandate.

21. Simran Singh, "Huron University College Professor Refuses to Abide by School's Vaccine Mandate in the Name of Ethics," *Toronto Star*, September 17, 2021, https://www.thestar.com/news/gta/2021/09/08/western-university-professor-refuses-to-abide-by-schools-vaccine-mandate-in-the-name-of-ethics.html.

22. Kit Knightly, "CDC Director: 'We May Need to Update Our Definition of 'Fully Vaccinated,''" *Off Guardian*, October 23, 2021, https://off-guardian.org/2021/10/23/cdc-director-we-may-need-to-update-our-definition-of-fully-vaccinated.

23. Kate McCann (@Kate McCann), "Have asked No10 to clarify the 'up to 90pc of patients in ICU are not boosted' figure and spokesman for PM says this is anecdotal evidence from "some NHS Trusts" which Boris Johnson was reflecting." Twitter, December 29, 2021, 5:51 a.m., https://twitter.com/KateEMcCann/status/1476143761243656197.

Chapter 3: Divide and Rule

1. Gluboco Lietuva (@gluboco), "Life under the EU's first strictly-enforced Covid Pass regime covering all society: Lithuania," Twitter, September 28, 2021, 7:21 a.m., https://mobile.twitter.com/gluboco/status/1442811790740578304.

2. The Office of the Government of the Republic of Lithuania, "COVID-19-Related Restrictions," *Korona Stop*, November 16, 2021, https://koronastop.lrv.lt/en/covid-19-related-restrictions-1.

3. "Lithuanian Government Adopts Slew of Restrictions for the Non-vaccinated," *LRT.lt*, August 11, 2021, https://www.lrt.lt/en/news-in-english/19/1466979/lithuanian-government-adopts-slew-of-restrictions-for-the-non-vaccinated.

4. Robin Wright, "The Story of 2019: Protests in Every Corner of the Globe," *The New Yorker*, December 30, 2019, https://www.newyorker.com/news/our-columnists/the-story-of-2019-protests-in-every-corner-of-the-globe.

5. Anne Gulland, "New Zealand Is Moving to a Two-Tier Society, but the Unvaccinated Are Already a Global Underclass," *The Telegraph*, October 25, 2021, https://www.telegraph.co.uk/global-health/science-and-disease/new-zealand-moving-two-tier-society-unvaccinated-already-underclass.

6. Rt Hon Jacinda Ardern, "New COVID-19 Protection Framework Delivers Greater Freedoms for Vaccinated New Zealanders," Beehive.govt.nz, October 22, 2021, https://www.beehive.govt.nz/release/new-covid-19-protection-framework-delivers-greater-freedoms-vaccinated-new-zealanders.

7. Anika Singanayagam et al., "Community Transmission and Viral Load Kinetics of the SARS-CoV-2 delta (B.1.617.2) Variant in Vaccinated and Unvaccinated

Individuals in the UK: A Prospective, Longitudinal, Cohort Study," *The Lancet*, October 29, 2021, doi:10.1016/S1473-3099(21)00648-4.

8. "COVID-19: Vaccine Passports Could Create 'Two-Tier Society,' Equality Watchdog Warns," *BBC News*, April 15, 2021 https://www.bbc.com/news/uk-56755161.

9. "Considerations for Potential Impact of Plan B Measures," Gov.uk, October 13, 2021, https://assets.publishing.service.gov.uk/government/uploads/system/uploads/attachment_data/file/1027586/S1393_SPI-B_SPI-M_EMG_Considerations_for_potential_impact_of_Plan_B_measures_13_October_2021.pdf

10. Thomas Fazi, "Italy's Vaccine Passport Power Grab: Is Draghi Embellishing a Crisis to Sidestep Democracy?" *UnHerd*, September 29, 2021, https://unherd.com/2021/09/italys-cynical-plan-for-vaccine-passports.

11. "*Burioni: 'Ora No Vax chiusi in casa come sorci'. Meloni: 'Questa non è scienza. Vergognoso'*" [Burioni: "Now No Vax Closed in the House Like Sorci." Meloni: "This Is Not Science. Shameful,"], *HuffPost* (Italian), July 24, 2021, https://www.huffingtonpost.it/entry/burioni-ora-no-vax-chiusi-in-casa-come-sorci-meloni-questa-non-e-scienza-vergognoso_it_60fbdadde4b05ff8cfc88f70; Luca Telese, @lucatelese, "*Molto sobrio Oliviero toscani: 'I No vacs sono sub-umani*'" [Very sober Oliviero Toscani: "No vacs are sub-human], August 11, 2021, 7:32 a.m., https://twitter.com/lucatelese/status/1425465204641603586; Alessandro Salusti, "*Alessandro Sallusti e i 'criminali no vax': chi sono i politici e i conduttori tv 'cattivi maestri'*" [Alessandro Sallusti and the 'no vax criminals': who are the politicians and TV hosts 'bad masters'], *Libero Quotidiano*, August 31, 2021, https://www.liberoquotidiano.it/news/commenti-e-opinioni/28506724/alessandro-sallusti-criminali-no-vax-chi-sono-politici-conduttori-tv-cattivi-maestri.html; Stefano Feltri, "*Escludiamo chi non si vaccina dalla vita civile*" [We Exclude Those Who Are Not Vaccinated from Civilian Life], *Domani*, last modified September 6, 2021, https://www.editorialedomani.it/idee/commenti/escludiamo-gli-evasori-vaccinali-dalla-vita-civile-green-pass-o5ooy74c; Redazione Roma, "*L'assessore alla Sanità del Lazio D'Amato: «No vax paghino i ricoveri» Rosato: «La sanità è diritto di tutti»*" [The Councilor for Health of Lazio D'Amato: "No Vax Pay for Hospitalizations" Rosato: "Health Is Everyone's Right"], *Corriere Della Sera*, https://roma.corriere.it/notizie/cronaca/21_agosto_31/d-amato-no-vax-paghino-ricoveri-rosato-la-sanita-diritto-tutti-6c069306-0a38-11ec-9ad8-3887e018c8c4.shtml; "Andrea Scanzi, "*il post choc: 'Se fossi Conte godrei nel farvi morire come mosche'. Bufera sul giornalista*" Andrea Scanzi, the shock post: "If I were Conte I would enjoy making you die like flies." Storm on the journalist], *Il Tempo*, October 27, 2021, https://www.iltempo.it/politica/2020/10/27/news/andrea-scanzi-post-facebook-se-fossi-giuseppe-conte-morire-mosche-matteo-salvini-bufera-25027607.

12. Jeffery Zients, "Press Briefing by White House COVID-19 Response Team and Public Health Officials," The White House, December 17, 2021, https://www.whitehouse.gov/briefing-room/press-briefings/2021/12/17

/press-briefing-by-white-house-covid-19-response-team-and-public
-health-officials-74.

13. Ziona Greenwald, "This Is How It Happens," *The Times of Israel*, December 14, 2021, https://blogs.timesofisrael.com/this-is-how-it-happens.

14. Jeffrey Barg, "Calling People 'the Unvaccinated' Could Be a Deadly Shift in Language," *The Philadelphia Inquirer*, September 1, 2020, https://www
.inquirer.com/opinion/the-unvaccinated-speech-noun-adjective-covid
-20210901.html.

15. Maggie Fox, "Unvaccinated People Are 'Variant Factories,' Infectious Diseases Expert Says," *CNN Health*, July 4, 2021, https://edition.cnn.com/2021/07
/03/health/unvaccinated-variant-factories/index.html.

16. Amanda Marcotte, "It's OK to Blame the Unvaccinated—They Are Robbing the Rest of Us of Our Freedoms," *Salon*, August 12, 2021, https://www.salon
.com/2021/08/12/its-ok-to-blame-the-unvaccinated--they-are-robbing-the
-rest-of-us-of-our-freedoms.

17. Michael J. Stern, "It's Time to Start Shunning the 'Vaccine Hesitant.' They're Blocking COVID Herd Immunity," *USA Today*, April 30, 2021, https://
eu.usatoday.com/story/opinion/2021/04/30/require-covid-vaccine-resume
-normal-life-herd-immunity-column/4886673001.

18. Akilah Hughes (@AkilahObviously), "Petition to call anti-vaxxers 'plague rats,'" Twitter, August 2, 2021, 2:21 p.m., https://twitter.com/akilahobviously
/status/1422261165321711617.

19. Gregory H. Stanton, "The Ten Stages of Genocide," Genocide Watch, last updated 2020, https://www.genocidewatch.com/tenstages.

20. Khaleda Rahman, "Vaccine Mandates Put Black Lives Matter Activists on Collision Course with Democrats," *Newsweek*, September 23, 2021, https://
www.newsweek.com/vaccine-mandates-black-lives-matter-activists-collision
-course-democrats-1631612.

21. Nambi Ndugga et al., "Latest Data on COVID-19 Vaccinations by Race/Ethnicity," *KFF*, November 17, 2021, https://www.kff.org/coronavirus-covid-19
/issue-brief/latest-data-on-covid-19-vaccinations-by-race-ethnicity.

22. Cydney Livingston, "Black Americans' Vaccine Hesitancy Is Grounded in More Than Mistrust," *Duke Research Blog*, April 8, 2021, https://researchblog.duke
.edu/2021/04/08/black-americans-vaccine-hesitancy-is-grounded-by
-more-than-mistrust.

23. Thomas H. Maugh II, "Eugene Saenger, 90; Physician Conducted Pivotal Studies on Effects of Radiation Exposure," *Los Angeles Times*, October 6, 2007, https://www.latimes.com/archives/la-xpm-2007-oct-06-me
-saenger6-story.html.

24. Brynn Holland, "The 'Father of Modern Gynecology' Performed Shocking Experiments on Enslaved Women," *History*, August 29, 2017, https://www
.history.com/news/the-father-of-modern-gynecology-performed-shocking
-experiments-on-slaves.

25. Yang Hu, "Intersecting Ethnic and Native-Migrant Inequalities in the Economic Impact of the COVID-19 Pandemic in the UK," *Research in*

Social Stratification and Mobility 68 (August 2020): doi:10.1016/j
.rssm.2020.100528.

26. Günter Kampf, "COVID-19: Stigmatising the Unvaccinated Is Not Justified,"
Lancet 398, no. 10314 (November 2021): 1871, doi: 10.1016/S0140-6736
(21)02243-1.

27. Christopher Leonard, "The Fed's Doomsday Prophet Has a Dire Warning
About Where We're Headed," Politico, December 28, 2021, https://www
.politico.com/news/magazine/2021/12/28/inflation-interest-rates-thomas
-hoenig-federal-reserve-526177.

28. Julius Krein, "The Value of Nothing: Capital versus Growth," *American Affairs*
5, no. 3 (Fall 2021): https://americanaffairsjournal.org/2021/08/the-value
-of-nothing-capital-versus-growth.

29. Yang Hu, "Intersecting Ethnic and Native–Migrant Inequalities in the
Economic Impact of the COVID-19 Pandemic in the UK," *Research in Social
Stratification and Mobility* 68, no. 100528 (August 2020), doi:10.1016/j
.rssm.2020.100528.

30. Alex Gutentag, "Revolt of the Essential Workers," *Tablet*, October 25, 2021,
https://www.tabletmag.com/sections/news/articles/revolt-essential-workers.

31. Edward Yardeni and Mali Quintana, "Central Banks: Monthly Balance
Sheets," Yardeni Research, December 2021, https://www.yardeni.com/pub
/peacockfedecbassets.pdf.

32. Harriet Habergham, "Global Banks' $170 Billion Haul Marks Most Profitable
Year Ever," *Bloomberg*, August 3, 2021, https://www.bloomberg.com/news
/articles/2021-08-03/global-banks-170-billion-haul-marks-most
-profitable-year-ever.

33. Alexandre Tanzi and Mike Dorning, "Top 1% of U.S. Earners Now Hold
More Wealth Than All of the Middle Class," *Bloomberg*, October 8, 2021,
https://www.bloomberg.com/news/articles/2021-10-08/top-1-earners-hold
-more-wealth-than-the-u-s-middle-class.

34. Chuck Collins, "Updates: Billionaire Wealth, U.S. Job Losses and Pandemic
Profiteers," *Inequality.org*, October 18, 2021, https://inequality.org/great
-divide/updates-billionaire-pandemic; Alex Starling, "Vaccine Passports Will
Segregate Society," *Reaction*, October 28, 2021, https://reaction.life/vaccine
-passports-will-segregate-society.

Chapter 4: Untold Consequences

1. Lucy Tobin, "The New David vs. Goliath Battle for Small Businesses: Getting
Hold of Cardboard," *Evening Standard*, December 14, 2021, https://www
.standard.co.uk/business/sme-supply-chain-issues-london-cardboard-martha
-brook-mighty-small-popcorn-shed-amazon-b971871.html.

2. Hillary Hoffower, Ben Winck, and Andy Kiersz, "The Supply-Chain
Disaster That Is Eating Christmas Is Being Driven by a Biden-Xi Conflict That
Many Are Overlooking," *Business Insider*, October 9, 2021, https://www
.businessinsider.com/supply-shortages-semiconductor-chips-crisis-us-china
-trade-war-biden-2021-10.

3. Greg Robb, "Backlog at Los Angeles Port Won't Ease until June, Chief Says," *Market Watch*, December 9, 2021, https://www.marketwatch.com/story /backlog-at-los-angeles-port-wont-ease-until-june-chief-says-11639070874.

4. Guy Platten, "The Supply-Chain Crisis Is a Labor Crisis," *New York Times*, November 17, 2021, https://www.nytimes.com/2021/11/17/opinion/supply -chain-labor-economy-covid.html.

5. Ryan Petersen, @typefast, "Yesterday I rented a boat and took the leader of one of Flexport's partners in Long Beach on a 3-hour of the port complex. Here's a thread about what I learned." October 22, 2021, 6:39 AM, https:// twitter.com/typesfast/status/1451543776992845834.

6. "California Ship Pileup Still Piling Up—But Out of Sight, over Horizon," *Hellenic Shipping News Worldwide*, November 25, 2021, https://www .hellenicshippingnews.com/california-ship-pileup-still-piling-up-but-out-of -sight-over-horizon.

7. Martin Arnold and Alexander Vladkov, "Europe's Trucker Shortage Becoming 'Extremely Dangerous," *Financial Times*, October 12, 2021, https://www.ft .com/content/e8ca2a08-308c-4324-8ed2-d788b074aa6c.

8. Reality Check Team, "How Serious Is the Shortgage of Lorry Drivers?" *BBC News*, October 15, 2021, https://www.bbc.com/news/57810729.

9. Ryan Johnson, "I Am a Twenty-Year Truck Driver, Part 2: How Truckers Are Paid," *Medium*, November 16, 2021, https://medium.com/@ryan79z28 /i-am-a-twenty-year-truck-driver-part-2-how-truckers-are-paid-de86ea419f2f.

10. Megan Leonhardt, "The Great Resignation Is Hitting These Industries Hardest," *Fortune*, November 16, 2021, https://fortune.com/2021/11/16 /great-resignation-hitting-these-industries-hardest.

11. Ronald J. Pugliese, Jr., "We Can't Ignore Vaccine Mandates as We Look into Labor Shortages," *Fortune*, November 9, 2021, https://fortune.com/2021 /11/09/biden-vaccine-mandates-labor-shortages.

12. Meredith Wadman, "Having SARS-CoV-2 Once Confers Much Greater Immunity than a Vaccine—But Vaccination Remains Vital," *Science Insider*, August 26, 2021, https://www.science.org/content/article/having -sars-cov-2-once-confers-much-greater-immunity-vaccine-vaccination -remains-vital.

13. "We'll Consult Members on What Action They Want to Take in Response to 3% Pay Award," *Royal College of Nursing*, July 21, 2021, https://www.rcn.org .uk/news-and-events/news/uk-nhs-pay-deal-a-bitter-blow-to-nursing-staff -in-england-210721.

14. Ben Wolfgang, "System Strained as Military Personnel Seek Religious Waivers from COVID-19 Vaccine," *Washington Times*, November 21, 2021, https:// www.washingtontimes.com/news/2021/nov/21/system-strained-military -personnel-seek-religious-.

15. Paul Gallagher, "NHS Waiting List: Heart Patients Facing up to Two-Year Delays for Vintal Scans," *iNews*, November 16, 2021, https://inews.co.uk /news/health/nhs-waiting-lists-heart-patients-facing-delays-vital -scans-1301750.

16. Chris Giles and Sarah Neville, "UK Enters Wave of Excess Deaths Not Fully Explained by COVID," November 23, 2021, https://www.ft.com/content /05e32f95-0e7e-4d2a-b408-6ec6035dea8e.

17. Lamorna Tregenza Reid, "The Government's Vaccine Mandate for Care Home Workers Will Do More Harm than Good," *Varsity*, November 23, 2021, https://www.varsity.co.uk/opinion/22506.

18. "UL Care Homes: How Are Staff Shortages Affecting You?" *The Guardian*, October 12, 2021, https://www.theguardian.com/society/2021/oct/12/uk -care-home-staff-how-are-labour-shortages-affecting-you.

19. Robert Booth, "Care Homes in England Set to Lose 50,000 Staff as COVID Vaccine Become Mandatory," *The Guardian*, November 10, 2021, https:// www.theguardian.com/world/2021/nov/10/care-homes-in-england-set-to -lose-50000-staff-as-covid-vaccine-becomes-mandatory.

20. Andrew Gregory and Robert Booth, "NHS Faces Bed Crisis as Care Homes Stop Taking Patients from Hospital," *The Guardian*, October 13, 2021, https://www.theguardian.com/society/2021/oct/13/nhs-faces-beds-crisis -as-care-homes-stop-taking-patients-from-hospitals.

21. Caroline Molloy, "Go Private for the Treatment You Need, NHS Tells Patients," *Open Democracy*, November 23, 2021, https://www.opendemocracy.net/en /ournhs/go-private-for-the-treatment-you-need-nhs-tells-patients.

22. Simon Little and Kamil Karamali, "B.C. Weighs Allowing COVID-19- Positive Health-Care Workers Back on the Job," *Global News*, December 29, 2021, https://globalnews.ca/news/8479456/bc-covid-19-positive -health-care-workers.

23. Aallyah Wright, "Biden's Vaccine Mandate Could Further Strain Rural Hospitals," *PEW*, October 21, 2021, https://www.pewtrusts.org/en/research -and-analysis/blogs/stateline/2021/10/21/bidens-vaccine-mandate-could -further-strain-rural-hospitals.

24. "Mount Sinai South Nassau Temporarily Closes Long Beach Emergency Department Due to Nursing Staff Shortages," *South Nassau*, November 22, 2021, https://www.southnassau.org/sn/current-news/mount-sinai -south-nassau-temporarily-closes-long-b-180.

25. Alia Paavola, "13 Hospitals Closing Departments, Ending Services," *Becker's Hospital Review*, December 3, 2021, https://www.beckershospitalreview.com /patient-flow/13-hospitals-closing-departments-ending-services.html.

26. Grégoire Sauvage, "*Pénurie de soignants : le modèle hospitalier français au bord de la ruptura*" [Shortage of Caregivers: The French Hospital Model on the Verge of Rupture], *France24*, October 29, 2021, https://www.france24.com /fr/france/20211029-p%C3%A9nurie-de-soignants-le-mod%C3%A8le -hospitalier-fran%C3%A7ais-au-bord-de-la-rupture.

27. Nick Corbishley, "Spain's Labor Office Hit by Massive Ransomware Attack as Unemployment Hits Four-Year High," *Naked Capitalism*, March 16, 2021, https://www.nakedcapitalism.com/2021/03/spains-employment-office -hit-by-massive-cyber-attack-as-unemployment-numbers-surge-toward -record-highs.html.

28. Sara Morrison, "How a Major Oil Pipeline Got Held for Ransom," *Vox*, June 8, 2021, https://www.vox.com/recode/22428774/ransomware -pipeline-colonial-darkside-gas-prices.
29. "NBP Cyberattack," *The Express Tribune*, November 2, 2021, https://tribune .com.pk/story/2327340/nbp-cyberattack.
30. "Heads of Mizuho Financial and Mizuho Bank to Quit over Glitches," *The Japan Times*, November 19, 2021, https://www.japantimes.co.jp/news /2021/11/19/business/corporate-business/sakai-mizuho-scandal.
31. "Singapore Regulator Warns DBS Bank over Prolonged Service Outage," *Financial Times*, November 25, 2021, https://www.ft.com/content/af544024 -1b92-4273-92a1-82a7d00f338d.
32. Alex Finnis, "Lloyds, Halifax and Bank of Scotland Down: Online Banking and App Not Working as Customers Get 'N/A' Messages," *iNews*, November 18, 2021, https://inews.co.uk/inews-lifestyle/money/saving-and-banking /lloyds-halifax-bank-of-scotland-down-online-banking-app-not-working-n -a-meaning-explained-1307003.
33. Jeff Parsons, "Barclays App Goes Down as Online Banking Outage Infuriates Customers," *Metro*, October 27, 2021, https://metro.co.uk/2021/10/27 /why-is-barclays-app-not-working-thousands-of-customers-hit-by -outage-15492229.
34. "What Is Cyber Polygon?" Cyber Polygon, last accessed December 18, 2021, https://cyberpolygon.com/about.
35. World Economic Forum, "A Cyber-Attach with COVID-Like Characteristics?" YouTube video, 1:41, January 18, 2021, https://www.youtube.com /watch?v=-0oZA1B3ooI.
36. "Event 201," Center for Health Security, last accessed December 30, 2021, https://www.centerforhealthsecurity.org/event201.
37. Lawrence Abrams, "The Wrrk in Ransomware—July 2nd 2021—MSPs Under Attack," *Bleeping Computer*, July 3, 2021, https://www.bleepingcomputer .com/news/security/the-week-in-ransomware-july-2nd-2021-msps -under-attack.
38. Jack Healy, "With Widespread Power Failuers, Puerto Rico Is Cash Only," *The New York Times*, September 29, 2017, https://www.nytimes.com/2017/09 /29/us/puerto-rico-shortages-cash.html.
39. Daniel Keane, "Heathrow in Chaos with 2-Hour Queues as Passport e-Gates Fail Again," *Evening Standard*, November 10, 2021, https://www.standard.co .uk/news/uk/heathrow-passport-e-gates-fail-queues-airport-b965476.html.
40. "Chapter 2. Democracy Health Check: An Overview of Global Trends," *Global State of Democracy Report 2021*, IDEA, last accessed December 18, 2021, https://www.idea.int/gsod/global-report#chapter-2-democracy-health -check:-an-overview-of-global-trends.

Chapter 5: Rules for Thee, Not for Me

1. ANSA Editorial Staff, "Roma e il G20 'Zona rossa' di 10 km e tiratori scelti" [Rome and the G20 'Red Zone' of 10 km and Sharpshooters], *Ait Speciali*,

October 28, 2021, https://www.ansa.it/sito/notizie/cronaca/2021/10/25
/roma-e-il-g20-zona-rossa-di-10-km-e-tiratori-scelti_d18cf760-7c2a-4b8a
-8a87-43540d9a5df3.html.

2. Darren Boyle et al., "Hypocrite Airways? Jeff Bezos's £48m Gulf Stream Leads
Parade of 400 Private Jets into COP26 Including Prince Albert of Monaco,
Scores of Royals and Dozens of 'Green' CEOs—as Huge Traffic Jam Forces
Empty Planes to Fly 30 Miles to Park," *Daily Mail*, November 1, 2021,
https://www.dailymail.co.uk/news/article-10152027/Hypocrite-airways
-Jeff-Bezoss-48m-gulf-stream-leads-parade-400-private-jets.html.

3. Neil Pooran, "COP26 Delegates Will Not Need Scottish Government's
COVID Vaccine Passport," *Glasgow Live*, October 5, 2021, https://www
.glasgowlive.co.uk/news/glasgow-news/cop26-delegates-not-need
-scottish-21771576.

4. Aubrey Allegretti, "Business Leaders Arriving in England Granted Exemption
from COVID Quarantine," *The Guardian*, June 29, 2021, https://www
.theguardian.com/world/2021/jun/29/business-leaders-arriving-in-england
-granted-exemption-from-covid-quarantine.

5. Emma Harrison, "Matt Hancock Quits as Health Secretary after Breaking
Social Distance Guidance," *BBC News*, June 27, 2021, https://www.bbc.com
/news/uk-57625508.

6. Luke Kemp, "The 'Stomp Reflex': When Governments Abuse Emergency
Powers," *BBC Future*, April 28, 2021, https://www.bbc.com/future/article
/20210427-the-stomp-reflex-when-governments-abuse-emergency-powers.

7. Giorgio Agamben and Valeria Dani, *Where Are We Now?: The Epidemic of
Politics* (Lanham, Maryland: Rowman and Littlefield, 2021).

8. "List of National Emergencies in the United States," *Wikipedia*, last modified
November 18, 2021, https://en.wikipedia.org/wiki/List_of_national
_emergencies_in_the_United_States.

9. Christopher Caldwell, "Meet the Philosopher Who Is Trying to Explain the
Pandemic," *The New York Times*, August 21, 2020, https://www.nytimes.com
/2020/08/21/opinion/sunday/giorgio-agamben-philosophy-coronavirus.html.

10. Natalie Huet and Carmen Paun, "Meet the World's Most Powerful Doctor:
Bill Gates," *Politico*, May 4, 2017, https://www.politico.eu/article/bill-gates
-who-most-powerful-doctor.

11. Klaus Schwab, "The Fourth Industrial Revolution: What It Means, How to
Respond," World Economic Forum, January 14, 2016, https://www.weforum
.org/agenda/2016/01/the-fourth-industrial-revolution-what-it-means-and
-how-to-respond.

12. Kenneth Haar and Brid Brennan, "COP26: Financiers of Polluters in
Charge," *Transnational Institute*, November 2, 2021, https://www.tni.org/en
/publication/cop26-financiers-of-polluters-in-charge.

13. "Corporate Capture of Global Governance: WEF-UN Partnership Threatens
UN System," *ESCR-Net*, last accessed November 18, 2021, https://www
.escr-net.org/news/2019/corporate-capture-global-governance-wef-un
-partnership-threatens-un-system.

14. Anne Quito, "Why Getting Rid of Paper Passports Might Be Good for Business," *World Economic Forum*, September 7, 2021, https://www.weforum.org/agenda/2021/09/passports-travel-work-digital.
15. Santiago Fernández de Lis et al., "Global Future Council on Responsive Financial Systems: Three Ways to Accelerate a Digital-Led Recovery," *World Economic Forum*, October 2021, https://www3.weforum.org/docs/WEF_GFC_Three_ways_to_accelerate_a_digital_led_recovery_2021.pdf.
16. Katherine Griffiths, "Small Firms Took on Huge Debt in Pandemic, Bank of England Says," *The Times*, October 9, 2021, https://www.thetimes.co.uk/article/small-firms-took-on-huge-debt-in-pandemic-bank-of-england-says-j9mfvlhq8.
17. Evelyn Cheng, "China's Tech Giants Generate Billions for Investors—but Small Businesses are Being Squeezed," CNBC, August 11, 2021, https://www.cnbc.com/2021/08/12/chinas-tech-giants-generate-billions-but-squeezed-small-businesses.html.
18. David Bol, "COVID Scotland: Business Leaders Warn Nicola Stugeon Vaccine Passports Risk Ruining Recovery," *The Herald*, September 3, 2021, https://www.heraldscotland.com/politics/19557086.covid-scotland-business-leaders-warn-nicola-sturgeon-vaccine-passports-risk-ruining-recovery.
19. "COVID: Scottish Vaccine Passport Scheme Could Be Expanded," *BBC News*, https://www.bbc.com/news/uk-scotland-scotland-politics-59225246.
20. Owen Hughes, "Wales's New COVID Passports 'Will Close' Some Venues, Says Welsh Hospitality Group," *Business Live*, September 17, 2021, https://www.business-live.co.uk/economic-development/waless-new-covid-passports-will-21599449.
21. Kerem Inal, "Supply Chain Problems Forcing Small Businesses to Change How They Operate," *ABC News*, October 24, 2021, https://abcnews.go.com/Business/supply-chain-problems-forcing-small-businesses-change-operate/story?id=80713564.
22. "NFIB: Over Half of Small Businesses Have Job Openings They Can't Fill," *WIS Business*, October 12, 2021, https://www.wisbusiness.com/2021/nfib-over-half-of-small-businesses-have-job-openings-they-cant-fill.
23. Joseph Choi, "Anti-Vaccine Protests Blamed for COVID-19 Outbreak in Italian City," *The Hill*, November 4, 2021, https://thehill.com/policy/international/europe/580026-anti-vaccine-protests-blamed-for-covid-19-outbreak-in-italian.
24. "*I 'No Green Pass' tornano in piazza. Bologna vieta manifestazioni fino al 9 gennaio*" [The "No Green Passes" Return to the Streets. Bologna Prohibits Demonstrations until January 9th], November 26, 2021, https://www.ilsole24ore.com/art/i-no-green-pass-tornano-piazza-bologna-vieta-manifestazioni-fino-9-gennaio-AEoCMTz.
25. Andrew Van Dam and Alyssa Fowers, "Two Forces Collided to Create the Most Unusual Job Market in Modern American History," *Seattle Times*, December 31, 2021, https://www.seattletimes.com/business/two-forces-collided-to-create-the-most-unusual-job-market-in-modern-american-history.

26. Iv Hendrix, "Officials Warn Vaccine Mandates Could Exacerbate Truck Driver Shortage," *The Hill*, November 4, 2021, https://thehill.com/homenews /house/580085-officials-warn-vaccine-mandates-could-exacerbate-truck -driver-shortage.

27. "Coronavirus No Longer the World's Top Worry as It Is Overtaken by Economic Concerns," *Ipsos*, October 26, 2021, https://www.ipsos.com/en-th /what-worries-world-october-2021.

28. Olivia Tam and Sofia Horta e Costa, "China Developers Confront a $197 Billion Challenge in January," *Bloomberg*, January 1, 2022, https://www .bloomberg.com/news/articles/2022-01-02/china-developers-confront-a -197-billion-challenge-in-january.

29. Wolf Richter, "After Blowing $4.5 Trillion on Share Buybacks, Airlines, Boeing, Many Other Culprits Want Taxpayer and Fed Bailouts of Their Shareholders," *Wolf Street*, March 17, 2020, https://wolfstreet.com/2020/03/17/after -blowing-4-5-trillion-on-share-buybacks-corporate-america-airlines-boeing -other-culprits-want-taxpayer-fed-bailouts-for-these-shareholders.

Chapter 6: A New Social Contract

1. Good Health Pass Collaborative, "Good Health Pass: A Safe Path to Global Reopening," last accessed December 18, 2021, https://idservice.com/content /dam/public/mastercardcom/idservice/pdf/Good-Health-Pass.pdf.

2. Gavi, "Donor Profiles," last accessed December 18, 2021, https://www.gavi .org/investing-gavi/funding/donor-profiles.

3. ID2020, "Imunization: An Entry Point for Digital Identity," *Medium*, March 28, 2018, https://medium.com/id2020/immunization-an-entry-point -for-digital-identity-ea37d9c3b77e.

4. "Identity in a Digial World: A New Chapter in the Social Contract," World Economic Forum, September 2018 https://www3.weforum.org/docs/WEF _INSIGHT_REPORT_Digital%20Identity.pdf.

5. Jacquie McNish and Liz Hoffman, "Mark Carney, ExBanker, Wants Bank to Pay for Climate Change," *The Wall Street Journal*, October 29, 2021, https:// www.wsj.com/articles/mark-carney-ex-banker-wants-banks-to-pay-for -climate-change-11635519625.

6. 1993 Global Leaders for Tomorrow, World Economic's Forum, list of participants, https://web.archive.org/web/20131203013754/http://www3 .weforum.org/docs/WEF_GLT_ClassOf1993.pdf; 1997 Global Leaders for Tomorrow, WEF, list of participants, https://web.archive.org/web /20140914231237/http://www3.weforum.org/docs/WEF_GLT_ClassOf 1997.pdf; 1998 Global Leaders for Tomorrow, WEF, list of participants, https://web.archive.org/web/20140914230101/http://www3.weforum.org /docs/WEF_GLT_ClassOf1998.pdf; 1999 Global Leaders for Tomorrow, WEF, list of participants, https://web.archive.org/web/20140914233005 /http://www3.weforum.org/docs/WEF_GLT_ClassOf1999.pdf; 2000 Global Leaders for Tomorrow, WEF, list of participants, https://web.archive .org/web/20130319042241/http://www3.weforum.org/docs/WEF_GLT

_ClassOf2000.pdf; "Community," The Forum of Young Global Leaders, last accessed January 11, 2022, https://www.younggloballeaders.org/community; and "Young Global Leaders," *Wikipedia*, last updated December 8, 2021, https://en.wikipedia.org/wiki/Young_Global_Leaders.

7. "Roadmap for the Implementation of Actions by the European Commission Based on the Commission Communication and the Council Recommendation on Strengthening Cooperation against Vaccine Preventable Diseases," European Commission, 2019, https://ec.europa.eu/health/sites/default/files /vaccination/docs/2019-2022_roadmap_en.pdf.

8. Jeffrey Dastin, "Amazon Scraps Secret AI Recruiting Tool That Showed Bias against Women," *Reuters*, October 10, 2018, https://www.reuters.com/article /us-amazon-com-jobs-automation-insight-idUSKCN1MK08G.

9. Derek O'Halloran and Manju George, "Identity in a Digital World—World Economic Forum," Good ID, January 13, 2019, https://www.good-id.org /es/articles/identity-in-a-digital-world-a-new-chapter-in-the-social-contract -world-economic-forum.

10. "Accenture Identity Solution Review," *Identity Review*, May 1, 2020, https:// identityreview.com/review/accenture-unique-identity-service-review.

11. ID2020, "ID2020 Alliance Launches Digital ID Program with Government of Bangladesh and Gavi, Announces New Partners at Annual Summit," *Cision PR Newswire*, September 19, 2019, https://www.prnewswire.com/news -releases/id2020-alliance-launches-digital-id-program-with-government-of -bangladesh-and-gavi-announces-new-partners-at-annual-summit -300921926.html.

12. "National COVID-19 Testing Action Plan," Rockefeller Foundation, April 21, 2021, https://www.rockefellerfoundation.org/wp-content/uploads/2020 /04/TheRockefellerFoundation_WhitePaper_Covid19_4_22_2020.pdf

13. "Initiative of the World Bank Group," The World Bank, last accessed December 18, 2021, https://id4d.worldbank.org/who-is-involved.

14. "The EU, the Externalisation of Migration Control, and ID Systems: Here's What's Happening and What Needs to Change," *Privacy International*, October 15, 2021, https://privacyinternational.org/long-read/4651/eu -externalisation-migration-control-and-id-systems-heres-whats -happening-and-what.

15. Carissa Véliz, "Why We Should End the Data Economy," *The Reboot*, June 4, 2021, https://thereboot.com/why-we-should-end-the-data-economy.

16. Zeynep Tufekci, "Think You're Discreet Online? Think Again," *The New York Times*, April 21, 2019, https://www.nytimes.com/2019/04/21/opinion /computational-inference.html

17. "Security Shortcomings in Patient Data System Apotti, Paper Report," *YLE*, July 24, 2019, https://yle.fi/news/3-10891713.

18. Noé Chartier, "Gov't Can't Be Trusted with Cellphone Tracking Amid Pandemic: Former Ontario Privacy Commissioner," *The Epoch Times*, December 29, 2021, https://www.theepochtimes.com/govt-cant-be-trusted-with -cellphone-tracking-amid-pandemic-former-ontario-privacy-commissioner.

19. "German Police under Fire for Misuse of COVID Contact Tracing App," *Deutsche Welle*, January 11, 2022, https://p.dw.com/p/45P8H.

20. Lauren Almeida, "NHS Deal Underlines Value of Health Data: Health Service Plans to Share GPs' Medical Records with Third Parties," *Investors' Chronicle*, June 3, 2021, https://www.investorschronicle.co.uk/news/2021/06/03/nhs -deal-underlines-value-of-health-data.

21. Madhumita Murgia, "England's NHS Plans to Share Patient Records with Third Parties," *Financial Times*, May 25, 2021, https://www.ft.com/content /9fee812f-6975-49ce-915c-aeb25d3dd748.

22. Graham Duggan, "12 Million OxyContin Pills Shipped to a Town of 500: How Profit Fuelled America's Opioid Crisis," *CBC*, November 12, 2021, https://www.cbc.ca/documentaries/the-passionate-eye/12-million-oxycontin -pills-shipped-to-a-town-of-500-how-profit-fuelled-america-s-opioid -crisis-1.6247359.

23. Madhumita Murgia and Max Harlow, "NHS Shares English Hospital Data with Dozens of Companies," *Financial Times*, July 26, 2021, https://www.ft .com/content/6f9f6f1f-e2d1-4646-b5ec-7d704e45149e.

24. Rob Davies, "NHS App Storing Facial Verification Data via Contract with Firm Linked to Tory Donors," *The Guardian*, September 15, 2021, https:// www.theguardian.com/society/2021/sep/15/nhs-app-storing-facial -verification-data-via-contract-with-firm-linked-to-tory-donors.

25. Nick Corbishley, "UK Goes Full-On Big Brother, Employs Facial Recognition Technology to Expedite School Lunch Queues," *Naked Capitalism*, October 22, 2021, https://www.nakedcapitalism.com/2021/10 /uk-goes-full-on-big-brother-employs-facial-recognition-technology-to -expedite-school-lunch-queues.html.

26. "Schools Pause Facial Recognition Lunch Plans," *BBC News*, October 25, 2021, https://www.bbc.com/news/technology-59037346.

27. "Biometrics," *EFF*, last accessed December 18, 2021, https://www.eff.org /issues/biometrics.

28. Bill Gates, "Making the World's Invisible People, Visible," *Gates Notes*, January 29, 2019, https://www.gatesnotes.com/Development/Heroes-in-the -Field-Nandan-Nilekani.

29. John Thornhill, "India's All-Encompassiong ID System Holds Warnings for the Rest of World," *The Financial Times*, November 11, 2021, https://www .ft.com/content/337f6d6e-7301-4ef4-a26d-a4e62f602947.

30. "The EU, the Externalisation," *Privacy International*, October 15, 2021, https://privacyinternational.org/long-read/4651/eu-externalisation -migration-control-and-id-systems-heres-whats-happening-and-what.

31. Tom Simonite, "The Best Algorithms Struggle to Recognize Black Faces Equally," *Wired*, July 22, 2019, https://www.wired.com/story/best-algorithms -struggle-recognize-black-faces-equally.

32. Zack Whittaker, "America's Small Businesses Face the Brunt of China's Exchange Server Hacks," *Tech Crunch*, March 10, 2021, https://techcrunch .com/2021/03/10/america-small-business-hafnium-exchange-hacks.

33. "Why Government Institutions Are the Perfect Target for Hackers," *Government Technology*, August 2, 2021, https://www.govtech.com/sponsored /why-government-institutions-are-the-perfect-target-for-hackers.

34. Stefan Boscia and Poppy Wood, "UK Vaccine Passport App Could Become 'Honeypot' for Hackers, Says Former Top Government Cyber Adviser," *City A.M.*, March 31, 2021, https://www.cityam.com/uk-vaccine-passport -app-could-become-honeypot-for-hackers-says-former-top-government -cyber-adviser.

35. "Regulation (EU) 2021/952 of the European Parliament and of the Council, Official Journal of the European Union, June 15, 2021, https://eur-lex.europa .eu/legal-content/EN/TXT/?uri=CELEX%3A32021R0953.

36. "COVID-19 Vaccines: Ethical, Legal and Practical Considerations," Parliamentary Assembly, January 27, 2021, https://pace.coe.int/en/files/29004/html.

37. "Digital Identity Document Validation Technology (IDVT)," GOV.UK, Coronavirus (COVID-19): Latest Updates and Guidance, December 27, 2021, https://www.gov.uk/government/publications/digital-identity -document-validation-technology-idvt.

38. Kristel Teyras, "How Digital ID Can Help Citizens Access Government Services from Anywhere," *Thales*, last updated December 1, 2021, https:// dis-blog.thalesgroup.com/identity-biometric-solutions/2021/07/27/how -digital-id-can-help-citizens-access-government-services-from-anywhere.

39. Jenn Markey, "Vaccine Passports, National ID's, Secure Credentials and Considerations for Building Trust in a Post-Pandemic World," *Entrust*, February 24, 2021, https://www.entrust.com/blog/2021/02/vaccine-passports -national-ids-secure-credentials-and-considerations-for-building-trust-in-a -post-pandemic-world.

40. Sikh For Truth (@SikhForTruth), "8 Jul 2020 – Biometric Digital ID for me is a very big part of the future"—Tony Blair . . .," July 27, 2021, https://twitter .com/SikhForTruth/status/1420057530651271170?ref_src=twsrc%5Etfw.

41. "Austria Says It Opposes EU Plan to Cap Cash Payments at 10,000 Euros," *Reuters*, July 15, 2021, https://www.reuters.com/article/us-eu -moneylaundering-austria-idUSKBN2EL15P.

42. Nobert Häring, "Defense Contractor Thales Calls Digital Vaccination Passes 'Precursor' to Universal Digital Indentification," *Money and More* (blog), August 30, 2021, https://norberthaering.de/en/power-control/thales-2.

43. Rachel King and Alice Shen, "Will Cash Survive COVID-19?," *Central Banking*, Marych 20, 2020, https://www.centralbanking.com/central-banks /currency/7509046/will-cash-survive-covid-19.

44. Stefan Gleason, "Bank of International Settlements Chief Talks 'Absolute Control,'" *Investing*, July 12, 2021, https://www.investing.com/analysis/bank -of-international-settlements-chief-talks-absolute-control-200591072.

45. Taylor Locke, "'Future of Money' Economist Says the End of Cash is Coming—Here's What Could Replace It," CNBC, November 11, 2021, https:// www.cnbc.com/2021/11/11/predictions-for-future-of-money-cbdcs -stablecoins-cryptocurrency.html.

Chapter 7: A Glimpse of the Future

1. Simina Mistreanu, "Life Inside China's Social Credit Laboratory," *Foreign Policy*, April 3, 2028, https://foreignpolicy.com/2018/04/03/life-inside-chinas-social-credit-laboratory.

2. Pete Hunt, "China's Great Social Credit Leap Forward," *The Diplomat*, December 4, 2018, https://thediplomat.com/2018/12/chinas-great-social-credit-leap-forward.

3. @France 24 English, "China ranks 'good' and 'bad' citizens with 'social credit' system," YouTube video, 4:36, May 1, 2019, https://www.youtube.com/watch?v=NXyzpMDtpSE.

4. Jessica Reilly, Muyao Lyu, and Megan Roberson, "China's Social Credit System: Speculation vs. Reality," *The Diplomat*, March 30, 2021, https://thediplomat.com/2021/03/chinas-social-credit-system-speculation-vs-reality.

5. Rogier Creemers, ed., "Planning Outline for the Construction of a Social Credit System (2014–2020)," *China Copyright and Media*, last updated April 25, 2015, https://chinacopyrightandmedia.wordpress.com/2014/06/14/planning-outline-for-the-construction-of-a-social-credit-system-2014-2020.

6. Wu Ling, "腾讯也有了信用分, 除了免押金骑摩拜还能干什么?" [Tencent Also Has Credit Scores. What Else Can You Do Besides Riding Mobike without a Deposit?], *Sohu*, July 8, 2017, https://www.sohu.com/a/162878300_114778.

7. Mara Hvistendahl, "Inside China's Cast New Experiment in Social Ranking," *Wired*, December 14, 2017, https://www.wired.com/story/age-of-social-credit.

8. Josh Chin and Gillian Wong, "China's New Tool for Social Control: A Credit Rating for Everything," *The Wall Street Journal*, November 28, 2016, https://www.wsj.com/articles/chinas-new-tool-for-social-control-a-credit-rating-for-everything-1480351590.

9. Nicole Kobie, "The Complicated Truth about China's Social Credit System," *Wired*, July 6, 2019, https://www.wired.co.uk/article/china-social-credit-system-explained.

10. Hvistendahl, "Inside China's Cast New Experiment in Social Ranking."

11. Creemers, "Planning Outline."

12. "Keeping Score: How Bad Is China's Social Credit System?" *Documentary Channel*, July 30, 2021, https://rtd.rt.com/shows/infobites-show/china-social-credit-system-surveillance.

13. "Keeping Score."

14. "China's Social Credit System: Fact vs. Fiction," *The Diplomat*, July 3, 2021, https://thediplomat.com/2021/07/chinas-social-credit-system-fact-vs-fiction.

15. Alexandra Ma and Katie Canales, "China's 'Social Credit' System Ranks Citizens and Punishes Them with Throttled Internet Speeds and Flight Bans if the Communist Party Deems Them Untrustworthy," *Business Insider*, May 9, 2021, https://www.businessinsider.com/china-social-credit-system-punishments-and-rewards-explained-2018-4.

16. Genia Kostka, "China's Social Credit Systems and Public Opinion: Explaining High Levels of Approval," *Sage Journals*, February 13, 2019, doi:10.1177/1461444819826402.

17. Eunsun Cho, "The Social Credit System: Not Just Another Chinese Idiosyncrasy," *Journal of Public and International Affairs*, last accessed December 17, 2021, https://jpia.princeton.edu/news/social-credit -system-not-just-another-chinese-idiosyncrasy

18. "Orwell's Nightmare: China's Social Credit System," *The Asian Institute for Policy Study*, February 28, 2017, http://en.asaninst.org/contents/orwells -nightmare-chinas-social-credit-system.

19. "China's Social Credit System: Fact vs. Fiction."

20. Liu Xuanzun, "Social Credit System Must Bankrupt Discredited People: Former Official," *Global Times*, May 20, 2018, https://www.globaltimes.cn /content/1103262.shtml.

21. Don Reisinger, "China Banned 23 Million People from Traveling Last Year for Poor 'Social Credit' Scores," *Fortune*, February 22, 2019, https://fortune .com/2019/02/22/china-social-credit-travel-ban.

22. Nathan Vanderklippe, "Chinese Blacklist an Early Glimpse of Sweeping New Social-Credit Control," *The Globe and Mail*, January 3, 2018, https://www .theglobeandmail.com/news/world/chinese-blacklist-an-early-glimpse-of -sweeping-new-social-credit-control/article37493300.

23. Sarah Young, "Chinese City Apologises after 'Shaming' People for Wearing Pyjamas in Public," *The Independent*, January 21, 2020, https://www .independent.co.uk/life-style/china-suzhou-pyjamas-shame-wear-public -photo-apology-a9294386.html.

24. Paul Bischoff, "Surveillance Camera Statistics: Which Cities Have the Most CCTV Cameras?" *Comparitech*, May 17, 2021, https://www.comparitech .com/vpn-privacy/the-worlds-most-surveilled-cities.

25. Jonathan Hillman, "China Is Watching You," *The Atlantic*, October 18, 2021, https://www.theatlantic.com/ideas/archive/2021/10/china-america -surveillance-hikvision/620404.

26. Liza Lin and Newley Purnell, "A World with a Billion Cameras Watching You Is Just Around the Corner," *The Wall Street Journal*, December 6, 2019, https://www.wsj.com/articles/a-billion-surveillance-cameras-forecast-to-be -watching-within-two-years-11575565402.

27. Bischoff, "Surveillance Camera Statistics."

28. Irina Ivanova, "Video Surveillance in U.S. Described as on Par with China," *CBS News*, December 10, 2019, https://www.cbsnews.com/news/the-u-s -uses-surveillance-cameras-just-as-much-as-china.

29. Samuel Woodhams, "London Is Buying Heaps of Facial Recognition Tech," *Wired*, September 27, 2021, https://www.wired.co.uk/article/met-police -facial-recognition-new.

30. Melissa Heikkilä, "Data Watchdog Warns Europe 'Is Not Ready' for AI-Powered Surveillance," *Político*, November 2, 2021, https://www.politico.eu/article /data-watchdog-europe-ai-surveillance-wojciech-wiewiorowski.

31. "EU: Artificial Intelligence Act: Council Aims to Simplify Use of Mass Biometric Surveillance by Law Enforcement," *Statewatch*, November 29, 2021, https://www.statewatch.org/news/2021/november/eu-artificial-intelligence-act-council-aims-to-simplify-use-of-mass-biometric-surveillance-by-law-enforcement.
32. Meredith Whittaker and Lucy Suchman, "The Myth of Artificial Intelligence," *The American Prospect*, December 8, 2021, https://prospect.org/culture/books/myth-of-artificial-intelligence-kissinger-schmidt-huttenlocher.
33. Maggie Throup et al., "New Pilot to Help People Eat Better and Exercise More," Gov.uk, October 22, 2021, https://www.gov.uk/government/news/new-pilot-to-help-people-eat-better-and-exercise-more.
34. "Carrot Rewards," *Wikipedia*, last updated November 9, 2021, https://en.wikipedia.org/wiki/Carrot_Rewards.
35. "Civil Rights Groups Demand AirBnB Reform Discriminatory Policy on Arrest and Conviction Records Use to Ban People from Platform," *ACLU*, September 23, 2020, https://www.aclu.org/press-releases/civil-rights-groups-demand-airbnb-reform-discriminatory-policy-arrest-and-conviction.
36. Shubham Verma, "WhatsApp Banned over 20 Lakh Users in October in India, Reveals Monthly Compliance Report," *India Today*, December 2, 2021, https://www.indiatoday.in/technology/news/story/whatsapp-banned-over-20-lakh-users-in-october-in-india-reveals-monthly-compliance-report-1883172-2021-12-02.
37. Mike Elgan, "Uh-oh: Silicon Valley Is Building a Chinese-Style Social Credit System," *Fast Company*, August 26, 2019, https://www.fastcompany.com/90394048/uh-oh-silicon-valley-is-building-a-chinese-style-social-credit-system.
38. Arnoud Boot, et al., "Financial Intermediation and Technology: What's Old, What's New?," (IMF Working Papers, International Monetary Fund, August 7, 2020), https://www.imf.org/en/Publications/WP/Issues/2020/08/07/Financial-Intermediation-and-Technology-Whats-Old-Whats-New-49624.
39. Dan MacGuill, "Did Twitter Prohibit Making an Accurate Claim About COVID-19 Transmission?" *Snopes*, December 17, 2021, https://www.snopes.com/fact-check/twitter-ban-covid-vaccine.
40. Sumeyya Ilanbey, "Victorian Bar President Slams 'Appalling' New Pandemic Laws," *The Age*, October 27, 2021, https://www.theage.com.au/politics/victoria/victorian-bar-slams-appalling-new-pandemic-laws-20211027-p593n8.html.
41. Jun Pang, "England and Wales's Police Bill Threatens Anyone with a Cause They Believe In," *Open Democracy*, December 6, 2021, https://www.opendemocracy.net/en/opendemocracyuk/the-uk-police-bill-now-threatens-anyone-with-a-cause-they-believe-in.
42. H.R.550, House Energy and Commerce Committee and Senate Health, Education, Labor, and Pensions Committee, Immunization Infrastructure Modernization Act of 2021, Representative Ann Kuster, H. Rept 117–178, January 28, 2021, https://www.congress.gov/bill/117th-congress/house-bill/550/text.

43. Ben Westcott, "China's Zi Jinping Is Pushing for a Global COVID QR Code. He May Struggle to Convince the World," *CNN*, https://edition.cnn.com /2020/11/23/asia/china-xi-qr-code-coronavirus-intl-hnk/index.html.

44. Jon Henley, "Majority of Public in Europe Support COVID Vaccine Passports— Survey," *The Guardian*, November 19, 2021, https://www.theguardian .com/world/2021/nov/19/majority-of-public-in-europe-support-covid -vaccine-passports-survey.

45. Paul Kingsnorth, "How Fear Fuels the Vaccine Wars," *UnHerd*, November 30, 2021, https://unherd.com/2021/11/how-fear-fuels-the-vaccine-wars.

46. Maïthé Chini, "COVID Safe Ticket Led to More Infections in Belgium, Says Expert," *The Brussels Times*, November 29, 2021, https://www.brusselstimes .com/belgium/195563/covid-safe-ticket-led-to-more-infections-in -belgium-says-expert.

47. Sam Jones, "Austrians Who Refuse Covid Jabs Face Fines of Up to €3,600," *Financial Times*, December 9, 2021, https://www.ft.com/content/b55d7b24 -cc0b-456b-aa02-c13498be8234.

48. Nadine Schmidt and Frederik Pleitgen, "Germany Locks Down Unvaccinated People, as Leaders Plan to Make Shots Compulsory," *CNN*, December 3, 2021, https://edition.cnn.com/2021/12/02/europe/germany -lockdown-covid-restrictions-intl/index.html.

49. Advanced Purchase Agreement SI2.838958, European Commission, 2020: 3, https://www.rai.it/dl/doc/2021/04/17/1618676613043_APA %20Moderna__.pdf.

50. "Vaccince Contracts/Transparency: Greens/EFA Group Submits Application to the ECJ to Claim Right to Access to Information by the EU Commission," press release, October 29, 2021, https://www.greens-efa.eu/en/article/press /vaccine-contracts-transparency.

51. "About Our Team: Management Team," Orgenesis, visited December 2021, https://orgenesis.com/team.

52. Markus Becker, "The European Commission Deletes Mass Amounts of Emails and Doesn't Archive Chats," *Speigel International*, December 11, 2021, https://www.spiegel.de/international/europe/a-new-controversy-erupts -around-ursula-von-der-leyen-s-text-messages-a-6510951f-e8dc-4468 -a0af-2ecd60e77ed9.

53. Sikh For Truth (@SikhForTruth), "Nails It: 'Clearly what we are witnessing right now is the Chinafication of Europe, what is happening in China with social credit scores & we are seeing the same . . .," November 25, 2021, https:// twitter.com/SikhForTruth/status/1463824931377012737.

Chapter 8: The Resistance Is Now (or Never)

1. "Israeli Vaccine Advisor: 'We Have Made Mistakes,'" *UnHerd*, January 18, 2022, https://unherd.com/thepost/israeli-vaccine-chief-we-have-made-mistakes.

2. Elena G. Sevillano, "¿Pandemia o endemia? Europa empieza a plantearse cómo convivir con el coronavirus" [Pandemic or Endemic? Europe Begins to Consider How to Live with the Coronavirus], *El País*, January 16, 2022,

https://elpais.com/sociedad/2022-01-17/pandemia-o-endemia-europa
-empieza-a-plantearse-como-convivir-con-el-coronavirus.html.

3. "World Health Assembly Aggress to Launch Process to Develop Historic
Global Accord on Pandemic Prevention, Preparedness and Response," World
Health Organization, December 1, 2021, https://www.who.int/news
/item/01-12-2021-world-health-assembly-agrees-to-launch-process-to
-develop-historic-global-accord-on-pandemic-prevention-preparedness
-and-response.

4. Simone McCarthy, "Pandemic Treaty to be Front and Centre at Landmark
WHO Meeting," *South China Morning Post*, November 28, 2021, https://
www.scmp.com/coronavirus/greater-china/article/3157663/pandemic-treaty
-be-front-and-centre-landmark-who-meeting.

5. Mathilde Androuët, "Parliamentary Questions: World Health Organization's
Relationships with Its Private Donors," European Parliament, April 17, 2020,
https://www.europarl.europa.eu/doceo/document/E-9-2020-002335
_EN.html.

6. Yanis Varoufakis, "Techno Feudalism Is Taking Over," *Project Syndicate*,
June 28, 2021, https://www.project-syndicate.org/commentary/techno
-feudalism-replacing-market-capitalism-by-yanis-varoufakis-2021-06.

7. "New UN Report: Hunger in Latin America and the Caribbean Rose by
13.8 Million People in Just One Year," *Pan American Health Organization*,
November 30, 2021, https://www.paho.org/en/news/30-11-2021-new
-report-hunger-latin-america-and-caribbean-rose-138-million-people
-just-one-year.

8. CJ Hopkins, "The Year of the New Normal Fascist," *CJ Hopkins* [blog],
December 16, 2021, https://cjhopkins.substack.com/p/the-year-of-the
-new-normal-fascist.

9. Belga, "La justice namuroise constate, en référé, l'illégalité du Covid Safe Ticket
en Wallonie: ce que l'on sait" [The Namur Justice Finds, in Summary Proceed-
ings, the Illegality of the Covid Safe Ticket in Wallonia: What We Know], *Le
Soir*, November 30, 2021, https://www.lesoir.be/409575/article/2021-11-30
/la-justice-namuroise-constate-en-refere-lillegalite-du-covid-safe-ticket-en.

10. Helen Lyons, "Covid Safe Ticket Is Legal, Wallonian Court Rules," *The
Brussels Times*, January 7, 2022, https://www.brusselstimes.com/belgium
-all-news/200684/covid-safe-ticket-is-legal-wallonian-court-rules.

11. "Qui est 'Notre bon droit', l'asbl qui multiplie les recours contre les mesures
sanitaires?" [Who is "Notre bon droit," the Non-profit Organization That
Multiplies the Remedies against the Sanitary Measures?], *Le Vif*, December 14, 2021, https://www.levif.be/actualite/belgique/qui-est-notre-bon
-droit-l-asbl-qui-multiplie-les-recours-contre-les-mesures-sanitaires/article
-normal-1502367.html.

12. Álvaro Soto, "El Supremo tumba el pasaporte covid para entrar en el ocio
nocturno" [The Supreme Knocks Down the COVID Passport to Enter
Nightlife], *El Correo*, August 18, 2021, https://www.elcorreo.com/sociedad
/salud/supremo-tumba-pasaporte-20210818170045-ntrc.html.

13. "COVID Passports in Spain: A Region-by-Region Breakdown of Where They Are Required, and for Which Activities," *El Pais*, November 26, 2021, https://english.elpais.com/society/2021-12-01/covid-passports-in-spain-a-region-by-region-breakdown-of-where-they-are-required-and-for-which-activities.html.

14. Dominic Penna, Lucy Fisher, and Maighna Nanu, "Boris Johnson Suffers Huge Rebellion as Almost 100 Tory MPs Vote against COVID Passports," *The Telegraph*, December 14, 2021, https://www.telegraph.co.uk/politics/2021/12/14/boris-johnson-news-covid-vaccine-passport-vote-tory-rebellion.

15. Penna et al, "Boris Johnson Suffers."

16. "COVID Passport Policy Lacks Scientific Evidence Base," UK Parliament, September 9, 2021, https://committees.parliament.uk/committee/327/public-administration-and-constitutional-affairs-committee/news/157355/covid-passport-policy-lacks-scientific-evidence-base.

17. Silkie Carlo (@silkiecarlo), "The end of Covid passes in England is a MON-UMENTAL victory for civil liberties & equality. . . . What separates us from much of the covid-ID-managed West is the . . . ," January 19, 2022, 2:29 PM, https://twitter.com/silkiecarlo/status/1483929594990374920.

18. Andrew Neil, "'It's Time to Punish Britain's Five Million Vaccine Refuseniks: They Put Us All at Risk of More Restrictions,' Says Andrew Neil. So Why Shouldn't We Curb Some of Their Freedoms?" *Daily Mail*, December 9, 2021, https://www.dailymail.co.uk/debate/article-10294225/Its-time-punish-Britains-five-million-vaccine-refuseniks-says-ANDREW-NEIL.html.

19. Kim Willsher, "France Deploys Police to Guadeloupe to Quell Violent COVID Protest," *The Guardian*, November 22, 2021, https://www.theguardian.com/world/2021/nov/22/france-cracks-down-on-guadeloupe-protests-over-covid-measures.

20. Robert Muller and Jan Lopatka, "Czechs Scrap Mandatory COVID-19 Jabs, Daily Cases Hit Record," *Reuters*, January 19, 2022, https://www.reuters.com/world/europe/czech-republic-reports-28469-new-cases-coronavirus-record-daily-tally-2022-01-19.

21. "COVID: Huge Protests across Europe over New Restrictions," *BBC News*, November 21, 2021, https://www.bbc.com/news/world-europe-59363256.

22. Paul Schreyer, "Die Protestwelle ist da" [The Wave of Protests Is Here], *Multipolar*, December 17, 2021, https://multipolar-magazin.de/artikel/die-protestwelle-ist-da.

23. "Monday Demonstrations in East Germany," Wikipedia, last updated December 16, 2021, https://en.wikipedia.org/wiki/Monday_demonstrations_in_East_Germany.

24. Marcel Leubecher, "Große Breite der Proteste bis in die kleinsten Ortschaften hinein" [Wide Range of Protests Right into the Smallest Towns], *Die Welt*, January 21, 2022, https://www.welt.de/politik/deutschland/plus236366631/Corona-Demos-Breite-der-Proteste-bis-in-kleinste-Ortschaften-hinein.html.

25. Marvin Ziegle, "Anti-Corona Protests Escalate, Riots in Several German Cities," *The Jerusalem Post*, December 14, 2021, https://www.jpost.com

/international/anti-corona-protests-escalate-riots-in-several-german
-cities-688695.

26. Andrew Griffin, "Telegram Could Be Shut Down in Germany, Government
Warns," *The Independent*, January 12, 2022, https://www.independent.co.uk
/tech/telegram-germany-shutdown-ban-far-right-b1991523.html.

27. Georg Ismar, "Wie der künftige Kanzler seinen Corona-Coup eingefädelt—
und einige verärgert hat" [How the Future Chancellor Orchestrated His
Corona Coup—and Angered Some], *Der Tagesspiegel*, December 1, 2021,
https://www.tagesspiegel.de/politik/die-ungewoehnliche-kamin-runde-wie
-der-kuenftige-kanzler-seinen-corona-coup-eingefaedelt-und-einige-veraergert
-hat/27852052.html.

28. "Germany Urges EU to Reduce Recovery Certificates' Validity to 90 Days,"
Schengenvisainfo News, January 27, 2022, https://www.schengenvisainfo
.com/news/germany-urges-eu-to-reduce-recovery-certificates-validity
-to-90-days.

29. Aude David, "Pass sanitaire : bientôt obligatoire en entreprise?" [Health Pass:
Soon Mandatory in Companies?], *Journal du Net*, December 20, 2021,
https://www.journaldunet.com/patrimoine/guide-des-finances-personnelles
/1502791-pass-sanitaire-vers-un-pass-vaccinal.

30. Jon Henley, "Macron Declares His Covid Strategy Is to 'Piss Off' the
Unvaccinated," *The Guardian*, January 4, 2022, https://www.theguardian
.com/world/2022/jan/04/macron-declares-his-covid-strategy-is-to-piss
-off-the-unvaccinated.

31. "Fact Sheet: Biden Administration Announces Details of Two Major Vaccination Policies," White House, November 4, 2021, https://www.whitehouse
.gov/briefing-room/statements-releases/2021/11/04/fact-sheet-biden
-administration-announces-details-of-two-major-vaccination-policies.

32. "Is the "Workaround" Working? Fourth Court Enjoins Biden Vaccine
Mandate," *Jonathan Turley*, December 8, 2021, https://jonathanturley.org
/2021/12/08/is-the-workaround-working-fourth-court-enjoins-biden
-vaccine-mandate.

33. Robbie Whelan and Melanie Evans, "Some Hospital Drop COVID-19
Vaccine Mandates to Ease Labor Shortages," *The Wall Street Journal*,
December 13, 2021, https://www.wsj.com/articles/some-hospitals-drop
-covid-19-vaccine-mandates-to-ease-labor-shortages-11639396806.

34. Ron Elving, "Week inPolitics: Biden Says There Is No Federal Solution to
the Pandemic," interview by David Gura, *Weekend Edition Saturday*, NPR,
January 1, 2022, https://www.npr.org/2022/01/01/1069610932/week-in
-politics-biden-says-there-is-no-federal-solution-to-the-pandemic.

35. "COVID News: New York Reports Record Number of New Cases as
Holiday Travel Ramps Up," *ABC Eyewitness News*, December 19, 2021,
https://abc7ny.com/new-york-record-covid-cases-holiday-travel
-tsa/11357973.

36. Paul Kingsnorth, "How Fear Fuels the Vaccine Wars," *UnHerd*, November 30, 2021, https://unherd.com/2021/11/how-fear-fuels-the-vaccine-wars/.

37. Douglas Busvine, "Moderna Hopes to Market Combined COVID and Flu Booster in 2023: Booster Would Also Protect Against RSV in Single Shot that Would be Administered Before Winter," *Politco*, January 17, 2022, https://www.politico.eu/article/moderna-hopes-to-market-combined-covid-and-flu-booster-in-2023.
38. Hannah Kuchler, "Bill Gates Warns of Pandemics Potentially Far Worse than Covid," *Financial Times*, January 18, 2022, https://www.ft.com/content/c1ab6cee-4f84-4a85-9c53-9f5f444359d4.
39. Yves Smith, "Covid: 'The Narrative Is Crumbling,'" *Naked Capitalism*, January 24, 2022, https://www.nakedcapitalism.com/2022/01/covid-the-narrative-is-crumbling.html.

INDEX

ABOUT THE AUTHOR

Gerard Sirera Blasco

NICK CORBISHLEY is a writer, journalist, teacher, and translator based in Barcelona. Formerly a senior contributing editor at the San Francisco–based economics and finance news site Wolf Street, he is currently a regular contributor to the US financial news and analysis blog *Naked Capitalism*, where he writes about financial, economic, and political trends and developments in Europe and Latin America. He also worked for many years at a well-respected business and economics journal in Spain. Nick is an occasional speaker (in English or Spanish) on economic, political, and geopolitical topics. Nick holds a BA in history from Sheffield University, speaks three languages (English, French, and Spanish) and is a regular visitor to his beloved country-in-law, Mexico.